Special Places

for the discerning traveler

In

CALIFORNIA, THE PACIFIC NORTHWEST

WESTERN CANADA AND

THE NORTHERN ROCKIES

By
Fred Nystrom and Mardi Murvin Nystrom

ACKNOWLEDGEMENTS

This book would not be possible without the financial support of two special people, Marj Hale and Claire Stuart. Thank you for your trust!. Special thanks to our children Chad,Tyler and Makenna, for their patience with us when we are "on the road" so often. A last, but not least, thanks to Betty Lu Murvin, Mardi's mom, for being available to help out with the family during our many trips.

Special Credits

Editorial assistance by Brandy K. Denisco and Lynn Brightwell Gardiner

Editing: Beth Stewart

Production by Linda Kowalsky, Technaprint, Issaquah, WA

Photographic Contributions

Joseph Sohm/ AllStock 6-7, **Eric Figge 15, David Young-Wolf 21, Tom Burt 27 & 29, Dana Holt 31 & 33**, Russell Abramham 39 & 41, Mark Gordon 43 & 45, John Vaughan 45, Jonathan Reichek 51, Christina Del Villar 53, George Gardner 61, Jim Beazley 63 & 65, Richard Fleig 73 & 75. John Swain 85, C.E. Pefley/ AllStock 94-95, Steve Wanke 107 & 109, Bob Pool 111 & 113, Bruce Forster 115 & 117, Don King 121 & 123, Doug Plummer 125 & 127 & 129, Carl Bischoff 135 & 137, Bob Peterson 143, Richard Ian Shopenn 155, Robert Pisano 157, Liz Hymans/ AllStock 164-165, Karl Spreitz 169 & 171, Jurgen Pockrandt 173 & 175, Miles Arsenault 183 & 185, John Fulker 187 & 189, Sandra E. Hill 191, James Randklev/AllStock 224-225, Jack Williams 229.

Copyright 1992

ISBN 0-936777-02-8

Library of Congress catalog Number: 92-64125

The rates shown in this edition are correct as of the time of printing. Please note that all rates are subject to change without notice.

Printed in U.S.A.

INTRODUCTION

Since our first edition seven years ago, our goal has been to search out, by incognito personal visits, independently owned lodging, restaurant and allied businesses that maintain a similar high level of quality, service and personal attention to the needs of their guests. While the ambiance of an urban hotel like The Heathman is different than that of a rural bed and breakfast like the River Street Inn, the level of personal caring and attention to your needs is consistently high. We do not include chains or formula restaurants.

We are often asked about what makes one place special while another, down the road with many of the same features, is not. After visiting thousands of places, we have come to realize that the critical ingredient is quite simple. It is not the amount of money spent per room, the quality of the antiques or even the expensive setting. The common trait that makes each of the places in this book special is that they all evidence a highly developed sense of hosting. A good host treats you as a welcome guest in his or her home. They see you as an individual who has a variety of wants, desires and needs. Their goal is to help you enjoy your time and come away with the feeling that you were well cared for. It really is that simple. In comparison, most of the hospitality industry has been schooled in how to efficiently process their guests from check-in to check-out. The outcome of this mentality is that the only part of the guest that is important is the amount of money they leave behind.

In a concerted effort to add only those few really well-hosted places, we took the step of creating a self-monitoring association consisting of the innkeepers and restaurateurs who were in our prior editions. They work with us to help select the new places to be added or those to be dropped if their quality goes down. This intense, professional peer scrutiny keeps the quality of those selected as a Special Place very high. This double selection process ensures that you have the best travel experience possible.

During my many years with Sunset Magazine, I was always impressed with the magazine's consistent approach to presenting truthful; accurate and reliable information. We try to take that same approach and give you a written and photographic representation as close to the real experience as possible. We hope you will enjoy discovering these Special Places as much as we have.

Fred and Mardi Nystrom

TABLE OF CONTENTS

California

EUREKA
FERNDALE
REDDING
GARBERVILLE
5
101
MENDOCINO
120
GUALALA
12
1
37
NAPA
SACRAMENTO
OAKLAND
SAN FRANCISCO
SANTA CRUZ
MONTEREY
CARMEL
1
SAN SIMEON
101
SOLVANG
SANTA BARBARA
LOS ANGELES
405
DANA POINT
5
SAN DIEGO
80
YOSEMITE NAT'L PARK
FRESNO
5
99

CALIFORNIA SPECIAL PLACES

A   Casa Tropicana

B   Blue Lantern Inn

C   Villa Rosa

D   Simpson House Inn

E   Alisal Guest Ranch

F   The Ballard Inn

G   Garden Street Inn

H   Martine Inn

I   Inn at Depot Hill

J   Babbling Brook Inn

K   Inn at Union Square

L   Washington Square Inn

M   Mansion at Lakewood

N   Wine & Roses Country Inn

O   Amber House

P   The Beazley House

Q   Napa Valley Balloons

R   Wine Country Inn

S   Silver Rose Inn

T   Belle de Jour

U   Whale Watch Inn

V   Stanford Inn

W   Gingerbread Mansion

X   Carter House and Hotel Carter

CASA TROPICANA INN

Address:	610 Avenida Victoria, San Clemente, CA 92672
Telephone:	(714) 492-1234
Location:	Overlooking the Pacific Ocean at San Clemente Pier
Hosts:	Rick and Christy Anderson
Room Rates:	$120 to $350 double; $15 per additional guest
Credit Cards:	American Express, Discover, MasterCard, Visa
Remarks:	Smoking is permitted outside on decks. Secure off-street parking provided.

Across the street from the Casa Tropicana you'll see the Amtrak train, the municipal pier and the Pacific Ocean. That's all. Set in the quiet costal community of San Clemente, this non-traditional bed and breakfast inn is ranked Number 2 in the state by *L.A. Magazine*. It's the place to go when you want to relax, watch the passersby and think of all the things you could do, if you wanted to."So many of our guests go out in the morning, tie their surfboards to their bicycles, and come back to their decks to eat breakfast before going over to the beach", notes owner Rick Anderson. "Later that afternoon, they're still there, the bikes haven't moved, and they have the most peaceful looks on their faces."

And that's just what Rick and his wife, Christy, intended when they bought the abandoned building that Rick transformed into the Casa Tropicana. A veteran building contractor, Rick saw the potential of this five-story building and spared no expense to create a "tropical paradise" that fulfilled his vision in every detail. He and Christy live at the inn with their two children. Christy applies her exceptional innkeeping skills to the inn's operation and to managing special events, such as business meetings and retreats, weddings and other gatherings of up to 80 people.

Imagining Islands

Outside, the Casa Tropicana reflects San Clemente's reputation as the "Spanish village by the sea." The smooth white plaster of the inn's exterior is accented by desert-colored Mexican tile stairs and a roof constructed of red tiles, hand-made for Rick in Tecate, Mexico. The nine rooms are named after different Paradise Island resorts and are designed around a corresponding theme with an astonishing attention to detail. All have refrigerators with ice-makers; most of the rooms have jacuzzis, decks and working fireplaces. A complimentary bottle of champagne welcomes you to your island refuge.

Designed to resemble a bamboo beach hut, the Bali Hai Room features a queen-sized waterbed with a mirrored thatch canopy. If you can pull yourself from the jacuzzi tub for two, you'll see the room also has a great ocean view. The romance of Bogart and Bacall is rekindled in the Key Largo Room, with its Casablanca fan, large jacuzzi and full tile floor. A king-sized bed with richly colored pillows sets off the crisp white of the room's large tiled fireplace. The Jungle Paradise is the largest suite, with cooking facilities, a fold-out leather couch, faux zebra-skin rugs and a floor-to-ceiling mural that lends the room a unique perspective. On the fifth floor is the deluxe Penthouse, which features a massive queen-sized oak bed, covered wet bar and a large bath with a three-sided fireplace and double headed shower. On a clear day, you can see from San Pedro to San Diego from the private jacuzzi on its large deck—great for those seeking perspective or finding it.

For Island Appetites

The fun and casual atmosphere of the inn extends to the Tropicana Grill, which offers a full bar and is located on the building's ground level. In addition to serving breakfast to guests and the public, the restaurant is open for lunch, dinner and an extravagant Sunday brunch. A life-sized alligator pours water into a cascading waterfall under a bamboo ceiling, and tropical birds call from their ringside quarters. Not the least of these attractions is the California-style fare you'll enjoy here, including Mexican specialties and other local favorites.

Breakfast for guests is also ordered right off the menu and may be served in the restaurant or in your room. Fajita omelettes, "Eggs San Clemente" and French apple French toast are among the morning choices and may be enjoyed with champagne or mimosas, if you like. Lunch and dinner feature fresh fish, pasta dishes, "Ragin' Cajun Garlic Ribs," steaks, salads and burgers.

Sea and Shore

Across the street from the Casa Tropicana is the San Clemente pier, flanked by a five-mile stretch of clean, sandy beach, with some of the best surfing and sunning in Southern California. All along the waterfront are shops and restaurants offering interesting wares and fares, ensuring an interesting stroll for wandering pedestrians. Tennis courts are located nearby, and if golf is your entertainment option of choice, visit the San Clemente municipal course. One of two in the area, the municipal course is the most played course in California and the second busiest in the country. For an even more eventful day, Disneyland is 45 minutes to the north. An easy day

The tranquil rooms overlook the beach and ocean.

long adventure is a trip to San Diego on Amtrak. Even with a trolley detour to Tijuana, you can be there and back for nachos in the afternoon. Amtrak also stops outside the Del Mar racetrack and inside Angel's Stadium, which is convenient for traveling sports spectators. Amtrak can be taken from most all parts of the country and ridden to the inn.

Getting There

From the north on Interstate 5, take the Avenida Palazada Exit and turn right. Turn left at the second light onto El Camino Real. Drive straight to Del Mar and turn right. Follow brown signs that direct you to the beach and pier.The inn is directly across from the pier. They will direct you to the parking area. From the south on Interstate 5, take the El Camino Real Exit, turn left. Continue to Del Mar and turn left. Follow brown signs to beach and pier.

BLUE LANTERN INN

Address:	34343 Street of the Blue Lantern, Dana Point, CA 92629
Telephone:	(714) 661-1304; FAX (714) 496-1483
Location:	Overlooking the Dana Point Yacht Harbor.
Host:	Tom Taylor, Innkeeper
Room Rates:	Rooms $135 to $250, depending on view; Tower Suite $350; includes gourmet breakfast, afternoon tea, wine and hors d'oeuvres
Credit Cards:	American Express, MasterCard, Visa
Remarks:	Children welcome. Handicapped accessible. No smoking.

Perched above the Dana Point Yacht Harbor with one of the best views in town is an enchanting Cape Cod bed-and-breakfast called the Blue Lantern Inn. Laced with romance and charm, the inn is a storybook hideaway of which every honeymooning couple dreams. The panoramic views of the Pacific, spectacular sunsets, dramatic accommodations and lovely park next door are all ingredients for a heavenly stay.

Cape Cod Charm

The inn reflects the Cape Cod theme of Dana Point with its gabled slate roof, cobblestone paths and flower borders. Its 29 lavish guests rooms are individually decorated with elegant, traditional furnishings and the soft colors of the coast — seafoam green, lavender, periwinkle and sand. Print wallpapers, patterned carpet and thick quilts create a joyful, romantic atmosphere. Each room offers a fireplace, large private bathroom with two sinks, jacuzzi tub for two, fluffy terry robes, a color television and refrigerator, complete with complimentary beverages. Almost all of the rooms have panoramic views of the Pacific and private terraces where you can enjoy the sunset or eat a leisurely breakfast. The Tower Suite, the ultimate in luxury, comes with a 20-foot vaulted ceiling, a king-sized bed and a breathtaking 180-degree view of the coast and harbor.

Each morning, guests awaken to a breakfast buffet of home-baked breads, muffins, cereals, fruit, hot entrees, juices and freshly brewed coffee. The afternoon brings tea, wine and hors d'oeuvres served with style in the spacious library. A fireplace, small bar, game tables and good reading light make the library a popular spot. Other little touches that we think make the Blue Lantern Inn special include an evening towel change and turndown service with chocolates, and an endless supply of fresh fruit and cookies.

In addition to the library, which will accommodate a gathering of 25 people, business travelers will appreciate the Blue Lantern's fully equipped exercise room and two conference rooms, one which seats up to six people, the other up to 10. A FAX machine, audiovisual equipment and catering services are also available.

Dana Point and the artsy community of Laguna Beach are home to interesting shops and art galleries. During June, "a must" is the Laguna Art Festival and The Pageant of the Masters, an extraordinarily impressive showcase of life-size renditions of famous fine art pieces using real people. There is also whale watching, sailing, windsurfing, deep-sea fishing and para-sailing for you thrill seekers.

Getting There

From the south, travel north on the Pacific Coast Highway (Highway 1) through Dana Point. Turn left onto the Street of the Blue Lantern. The inn is on your right at the dead end. From the north, travel five miles south of Laguna Beach on the Pacific Coast Highway. As you approach Dana Point, take a right onto the Street of the Blue Lantern.

The Tower Suite offers panoramic views of the Pacific.

VILLA ROSA

Address:	15 Chapala, Santa Barbara, CA 93101
Telephone:	(805) 966-0851; FAX (805) 962-7159
Location:	One block off the beach, near Stearns Wharf
Hosts:	Beverly Kirkhart, Owner/Innkeeper; Annie Puetz, Assistant Innkeeper
Room Rates:	$90 to $190 double on weekends and summer. Two-night minimum on weekends and holidays. $80 to $160 weekdays in winter.
Credit cards:	American Express, MasterCard, Visa
Remarks:	Rates include Continental breakfast, complimentary wine and cheese, evening port and sherry. Children over 14 welcome. No pets.

Blue ocean views from private verandas, palm trees, avocado groves and a sensual evening breeze make the Villa Rosa an enchanted place that is woven into the colorful tapestry of Santa Barbara.

Immediately upon entering Santa Barbara, you are aware that this is no ordinary beach town.The thing that sets the different cast is the architecture. The thick adobe walls with deeply recessed doors and windows, the graceful balconies and loggias and the red tiled roofs are all reminiscent of villages along Spain's Mediterranean coast. Perhaps this should be expected since Santa Barbara was under Spanish and Mexican control from 1782 until 1846. However there is little left from that period. After the 1925 earthquake, the Architectural Board of Review decided to promote the Spanish Colonial look, which can now be appreciated throughout the town.

Preserving The Past

In keeping with the preservation spirit, many of the centrally located historic hotels are being restored to their former elegance. The Spanish Colonial Revival Villa Rosa was built in 1931 and known for years as the "Hilton-by the-Sea". During its many years, the building was used as an apartment house, a motel and as off-campus housing for students. The decline in fortunes for the building continued until Beverly Kirkhart accepted the challenge and purchased the 9,000-square-foot building in 1981.

Transforming the dilapidated building into an immaculate 18-room inn was no easy feat. The total interior was gutted, the foundation rehabilitated and a completely new tile roof installed. Beverly's archi-

tectural creativity continued as she had the courtyard enclosed, added a solar heated pool and jacuzzi and created space for small meetings. Beverly's decorating skills came to play in furnishing the rooms in a Spanish Colonial style with the flair of the Southwest.

Beverly's restoration and the hospitality the guests receive has made Villa Rosa one of our favorite places to spend a few quiet days relaxing. Morning walks, afternoon beach times and early evening around the secluded pool are important parts of our visit.

Villa Perfecta

We have heard contented guests refer to the inn as "Villa Perfecta." This term aptly describes this romantic retreat that is steeped in relaxed elegance. Guests who stay receive a range of amenities that would be found in a European resort and the personalized pampering of a domestic bed and breakfast inn.

The pale pink, two-story building presents a facade of visual diversity- turreted corners, cupolas, arched porticos and wrought iron balconies. Views of the beach, Stearns Wharf and mountains lining the south coast are rewarding sights from the inn. In typical Spanish tradition, there is also a serene garden courtyard complete with spa and pool.

There is an instant sense of belonging as guests are greeted into the living room by Beverly or Annie. A few moments in front of the magnificent fireplace with a mug of freshly brewed coffee or a refreshing glass of wine may introduce thoughts of never leaving.

The rooms are decorated with Spanish and Mexican art and exotic potted plants. The terracotta-tiled baths add to the Mediterranean feel. The villa's signature rose graces the pillow on your bed. Three rooms include small kitchen facilities ideal for longer stays. Four deluxe rooms feature fireplaces and sitting areas ideal for relaxing with a good book. All rooms have telephones. Televisions are available on request.

Flair Without Fanfare

A complimentary breakfast of croissants, muffins, fruit and freshly brewed coffee is served in the sitting room. In-room or poolside service can be arranged by request. Wine, cheese and social congenialities are found in the living room from 5 p.m. to 7 p.m.

The conference room is an ideal site for small workshops and executive retreats. It offers professional conveniences in a quiet setting. For a quick break, the pool is just outside the glass doors.

Many of the cool rooms overlook the courtyard pool.

High Energy Or Relaxation

Santa Barbara is currently in the midst of a spirited revival of the cultivated arts. Always a big music town, it is also home to California's oldest continually running cinema house—the Lobero Theater. Take a trolley ride to the mission, the zoo or a historic museum. Or rent a bike and follow the coastline. Be it active or passive, Santa Barbara offers choices that appeal to both.

Getting There

From the north take US 101 south to Castillo Street. Turn right at the stoplight and follow Castillo Street to Cabrillo Blvd. Turn left at the stoplight and follow Cabrillo Blvd. to Chapala Street. Turn left on Chapala and the Villa Rosa is on the left side of the street. From the south, take US 101 north to Cabrillo Blvd. Exit. Turn left at the stop sign and follow Cabrillo Blvd. to Chapala Street. Turn right on Chapala and the inn is on the left.

SIMPSON HOUSE INN

Address:	121 E. Arrellaga Street, Santa Barbara, CA 93101
Telephone:	(805) 963-7067; toll free (800) 676-1280; FAX (805) 564-4811
Location:	In residential neighborhood
Hosts:	Glyn and Linda Davies, Gillean Wilson
Room Rates:	$85 to $200 double
Credit Cards:	American Express, Discover, MasterCard, Visa
Remarks:	No smoking and no pets are permitted inside the inn. Complimentary wine and hors d'oeuvres, bicycles, English croquet, beach towels and chairs.

Traveling to the Simpson House Inn in Santa Barbara is considerably easier today than it was when the house was built in 1874. Although modernization of travel has rendered the inn easily accessible, once you've entered its hedge-lined interior, you'll forget all about the 20th century.

Glyn and Linda Davies purchased the Simpson House, one of the oldest wooden buildings in Santa Barbara and in 1985 the Simpson House Inn was created. "From the start," Glyn says, "we all had a vision of preserving this old house as a piece of living history." With partner, Gillean Wilson (who, like Glyn, is from England), the Davies have woven a sense of permanence into the inn with antiques, original art and fine Oriental carpets.

A Houseful of Heritage

In the halls and stairways of the landmark inn, the Davies historic family photos are displayed. In the downstairs sitting room, historical books and photo albums are open for fireside investigation. The formal dining room, with large windows overlooking the garden, is an ideal setting for meetings and retreats of up to 25 people.

The six rooms inside the Simpson House are named in honor of Robert Simpson family, its original owner. Each has a private bath and is furnished with antiques, including such authentic accents as a Victorian pull-chain toilet and a Boston rocking chair. Most have brass beds and old-fashioned claw-foot tubs. In the summer of 1992, four spacious guest rooms were opened in the fully reconstructed barn behind the inn. Rooms have private decks and baths, fireplaces, pine floors covered with Oriental rugs, and antique pine armoires conceal televisions and VCRs.

Breakfast is served on the veranda, which overlooks the sunlit garden. Begin with yogurt, a variety of fresh fruits and cereal, or home made granola from the cereal bar. Strawberry blintzes or French toast made with fresh apples, baked and covered with caramel syrup, may be among the entrees that follow. "Then spoon homemade lemon curd over scones hot from the oven and add a bit of whipped cream," Gillean directs, "It's heaven."

Beyond The Gate

The Simpson House Inn is located within walking distance from many local attractions. On foot, you can explore the Museum of Art , the Alice Keck Gardens and Alameda Park, or walk through the historic downtown area.

Getting There

From the south on Highway 101, take the Garden/Laguna St. Exit and turn right onto Garden St. Go one block to Guittierez, turn left and one block to Santa Barbara Street., turn right. Continue on for 13 blocks to Arrellaga, turn left. The Simpson House Inn is mid-street on your right. From the north, take the Mission St. Exit and turn left onto Mission St. Drive six blocks to Anacapa St., turn right. Continue for four blocks to Arrellaga St., turn left.

The Simpson House is Victorian elegance secluded in an acre of gardens.

ALISAL GUEST RANCH

Address: 1054 Alisal Road, Solvang, CA 93463
Telephone: (805) 688-6411; FAX (805) 688-2510
Location: North of Santa Barbara in the Santa Ynez Valley
Host: Jack Austin, General Manager
Room Rates: $255 studio; $295 two-room suite. Rates based on double occupancy. Two-night minimum. Special packages available from September to June.
Credit Cards: American Express, MasterCard, Visa
Remarks: Rates include breakfast and dinner. All rooms have wood-burning fireplaces. No pets, bicycles or skateboards.

Surrounded by gently rolling hills that are golden in the summer and emerald green with splashes of wildflowers in the spring, the Alisal Guest Ranch is nestled in the secluded, scenic Santa Ynez Valley. The ranch's 10,000 acres are generously populated with eagles, hawks, deer, and occasional coyotes and mountain lion. Huge century-old live oaks dot the hillsides, but it is the sycamores that gave the place its name. In Chumash, Alisal means "grove of sycamores." The Native Americans named the area after the number of sycamores that they found in the valley.

The present owners, the Jackson family, acquired the Alisal in 1943. It soon became popular as a family gathering place, and a getaway for corporate executives and entertainment celebrities. The Jacksons have continued the tradition of California ranch life. They maintain the property as a working cattle ranch where some 2,000 calves are fattened each winter.

Private Retreat

Only 40 miles north of Santa Barbara, the Alisal Guest Ranch is not a dude ranch where visitors participate in chores, but rather a private retreat that captures the feeling of living on a large, working ranch. It occupies approximately 350 acres of the land and can accommodate about 200 guests.

Guest cottages are clustered around manicured lawns and are decorated in simple motifs. The ranch has recently removed three old buildings and replaced them with two new units, each comprised of two studios and a suite. Bungalows that line the entrance to the ranch have front porches, two and three bedrooms, and large living rooms. Studios and two-room suites can be arranged for either king or twin beds. All have working fireplaces, which the Alisal staff

keeps well stocked with firewood. An exciting addition to the Alisal's fully-equipped conference facility is a beautiful 1,500-square-foot Hospitality House. It features a central living room suite surrounded by three separate studio rooms, all with private entrances.

Fun and Frivolity

A ride into oak-studded hills will tempt even the slickest of the city slickers. Two-hour guided trail rides into the hills are scheduled each morning and afternoon; lessons are available. Our favorite is the breakfast ride out to the old "adobe". Upon arrival, the crew prepares a hearty meal of eggs, flapjacks and other warm goodies around the open fire. Once back to the ranch, you can wash off your trail dust with a dip in the large, free-form pool.

The ranch has two golf courses. The original is a 6,286-yard, par 72 golf course, designed by Billy Bell. It is one of the ranch's main attractions, and is available to guests for a nominal daily fee. It utilizes the natural terrain, the sycamores and the live oaks to create a challenging championship course. A resident PGA pro is on staff. A fully equipped pro shop, lounge and restaurant make the package complete. New to the ranch is a second 18-hole public golf course designed by Helsey and Daray. The course, with its four lakes and club house is scheduled for completion in the fall of 1992.

It tennis is more your game, you'll be glad to hear of the seven championship tennis courts and pro shop. The resident teaching pro and assistants are there to assist and arrange tournaments. Lessons are enhanced by videotaped analysis.

The Alisal even has its own 100-acre lake, with sailing, rowing and windsurfing. The lake is stocked with bluegill, catfish and large-mouth bass. Since the lake is on private land, there is no license requirement and the ranch will supply you with tackle.

Rest and Relaxation

Dining at the Alisal is not typical of rustic ranch life. In the Ranch Room, the chef offers California cuisine at its best. You can eat as little or as much as you like. The menu is different for every day, so you won't tire of the same selections. Start with smoked salmon mousse on parmesan toast, freshly baked bread, and a superb caesar salad or the popular homemade tortilla soup. Fill a hearty appetite with roasted rack of lamb or tenderloin of beef with spicy red pepper coulis. Or choose the lighter fare of fresh salmon, swordfish, Santa Barbara shrimp, or the grilled and steamed vegetable plate served with fresh pasta. Dinner at the Alisal isn't complete without a slice of its famous oatmeal pie piled high with homemade

The quiet and private rooms are ideal for relaxing.

vanilla ice cream. In the warmth of summer evenings the ranch often does barbecues with live entertainment.

Summer is peak season when families come to stay for a week or more. But the beauty of the hills in spring and the trees in the fall make visiting Alisal special anytime of the year. Our preferred time is in winter, with clear sunny days and no crowds in the valley.

The Alisal is located near the picture-book town of Solvang, a charming little Danish community with restaurants, shops, services and world-renown Danish pastries.

Getting There

Airline service is available to Santa Barbara 40 miles away. By car, take Highway 101 to the Solvang/Lompoc Exit (Highway 246). Go east through Buellton for three miles to Solvang. Turn right on Alisal Road, past the golf courses to the Alisal's main entrance.

BALLARD INN

Address:	2436 Baseline Avenue, Ballard, CA 93463
Telephone:	(805) 688-7770; toll free (800) 638-2466
Location:	In the heart of the Santa Barbara Wine Country
Hosts:	Steve Hyslop and Larry Stone
Room Rates:	$155 to $185 double. Full breakfast included.
Credit Cards:	American Express,MasterCard, Visa
Remarks:	Seven-day cancellation notice required. Two-night minimum stay over a Saturday. Complimentary afternoon wine and hors d'oeuvres. Children are welcome with well-behaved parents. No smoking inside the inn.

Just 40 minutes from Santa Barbara, yet nestled in a country neighborhood of orchards and vineyards, the Ballard Inn offers an intimate country retreat from the strains of city living. Located in the center of the tiny township of Ballard, in the Santa Ynez Valley, this modern 15 room country inn is close to everything the country has to offer: quiet strolls past wandering geese and horses, smelling the blossoms in the apple orchards, sampling the newest harvest at one of the world renowned wineries, or bicycle rides and picnicking amidst some of the best wildflower displays in the spring.

Comfortable Elegance

Guests arriving at the two-story inn pass through flowering gardens framing a covered veranda with comfortable white wicker furniture. Once inside, to the right is a stunning three-sided fireplace of Green Italian Marble, while on the left is a hand-polished oak staircase cascading from the second floor. Subtle lights play off the marble from the large English brass and crystal chandelier above the entry. Here one of the friendly staff will greet you with a personal tour of the four common rooms, open to all the guests.

The living room is flanked by a large warming fireplace and softened with floral linen sofas and pillows, perfect for reading and relaxing. Antique cabinets display award-winning local wines and winery information. The photo album on the burl coffee table chronicles the stays of other happy guests, many on their third or fourth visit. The Vintners Room is a comfortable meeting room, where outstanding food and wine are served to guests each afternoon. The adjoining Stagecoach Room has a round table for games and cards and a soft leather sofa in the perfect spot for watching the big screen television. The large and cheery dining room, featuring antique oak furniture and white and pastel tablecloths, is often used for special parties.

Because of the exceptional size and comfort of the common rooms, the entire inn is frequently used for wedding parties, corporate executive meetings, family reunions and gatherings.

Historical Character

Each of the Ballard Inn's 15 guest rooms possesses it own special charm and character, reflecting the local history of the Santa Ynez Valley and its residents. All the rooms have California King-sized beds(longer than regular kings), Queen, or twin-sized beds; private baths and individually controlled air conditioning and heating. Seven rooms have fireplaces and several offer cozy down comforters. The Vineyard Room celebrates the local winemakers with a colorful grapevine print, chinz comforter on a California King-sized bed with a Willow headboard. The matching willow chairs and table, in a lighted setting are perfect for either sipping some of the Ballard Inn Chardonnay, or if you must, getting some business done. Through the windows are views of the local mountains or the nearby intimate Ballard Chapel. The Mountain Room, our personal favorite, is decorated in warm earth tones and offers stunning mountain views from its own balcony. Inside, the romantic setting is enhanced by the ready to use fireplace, comforter covered king-sized bed and plenty of relaxing space. The inn keeps all the rooms open for tour, when not occupied, so you can choose the room for your next stay. While telephones are not normally found in the rooms, should you require, one will be provided.

Special attention is paid to the food served at the Ballard Inn, as owners Steve Hyslop and Larry Stone have been in the restaurant business, as well, for many years. At 5 p.m., guests are treated to a tasting of great local wines served with speciality hors d' oeuvres. Mornings at the inn brings a full breakfast, cooked to order and served in the dining room, all included with your stay.

Great Chardonnay

The word is getting out: World-class wines are being produced in the Santa Barbara Wine Country; and the Ballard Inn is located right in the middle of all the most interesting places to visit and sample. Steve and Larry and their families have traveled through wine countries domestically and abroad staying in remote country inns, "We stayed in places that took really good care of their guests, and took pride in doing so," explains Steve. "We bought the Ballard Inn, and now we provide that special attention for people exploring this area." They have developed excellent relationships with the area's wineries and can arrange for special tours or tastings for you.

Bicycle riding has become as big a part of the Santa Ynez Valley as the wineries. The inn can make mountain bikes available, or you

The wide veranda is a perfect place to sit and relax.

can bring your own. There is a covered and secure bike rack at the inn for storage. Ride out to Figueroa Mountain, which, in the spring, turns orange with California poppies and lupine; or choose from several itineraries available from the inn's staff. Exceptional golf facilities are within 30 minutes of the Ballard Inn, and a new course at the Alisal Ranch will be open to guests of the inn in late 1992.

April is the time for the Carriage Classic, in which area horse breeders exhibit their thoroughbred horses in a parade of carriages at Firestone Ranch. At nearby Lake Cachuma, you can take an "eagle cruise" to nesting and sighting areas for golden eagles.

Getting There

From Highway 101, take the Solvang Exit . Follow Route 246 E. through Solvang to Alamo/Pintado Road, turn left. Drive three miles to Baseline Avenue, turn right. The Ballard Inn is 50 yards down the street to your right.

GARDEN STREET INN

Address: 1212 Garden Street, San Luis Obispo, CA 93401
Telephone: (805) 545-9802
Location: In historic San Luis Obispo
Hosts: Dan and Kathy Smith
Room Rates: $90 to $120 rooms; $140 to $160 suites
Credit Cards: American Express, MasterCard, Visa
Remarks: Two-night minimum stay on holidays and special event weekends. Rates include full breakfast and complimentary wine and cheese. Inappropriate for children under 16. No smoking. No pets.

In its location on the central coast of California, the city of San Luis Obispo is surrounded by grand mountain ranges and vast ocean beaches. Despite its population of 50,000 people, downtown San Luis Obispo has retained its old-fashioned charm, inspired by small shops and restaurants owned by residents. Among these locally owned establishments is the Garden Street Inn, owned and operated by Dan and Kathy Smith, and Mozart, the resident Lhasa/ Cocker mix and music aficionado.

Built in 1887, the Garden Street Inn has played an important part in the history of the town, and is listed on San Luis Obispo's "Heritage Home Inventory." Originally a single-family home, the building served as an apartment building, primarily housing students and singles, from 1920 until Dan and Kathy purchased it in 1989. Enhancing the Queen Anne and Italianate features of the house, the Smiths "renovated everything, except the charm," notes Dan.

Past, Present and Future

Each of the inn's rooms reflect people and places that have special significance to Kathy and Dan. Kathy explains, "We're sharing part of our lives with our guests, not just a room." The Goldtree Library is named for the Goldtree family, local merchants and wine-makers who were responsible for the developing of Higuera Street into the town's major thoroughfare. The upper reaches of the library's floor-to-ceiling bookshelves are accessible by ladder, and a crackling fire in the fireplace encourages settling into a good story. Many of the books were given as wedding gifts to Dan and Kathy who requested a book from each friend's personal collection.

Breakfast is served in the McCaffrey Morning Room, named for the second owners and local brewers who helped to establish San Luis Obispo. This sit-down meal includes fresh fruit, homemade breads

and muffins, and hot entrees such as crab souffle, Santa Clara quiche and "Featherbed Eggs". Coffee, tea and juice complete the morning fare.

By involving guests in their personal history and that of the town, the Smiths hope to inspire a sense of connection that will "help them to walk away feeling like their lives have been enriched." Kathy continues, "I give everyone a hug before they leave—it's like saying goodbye to a relative."

More Than a Bed

The Garden Street Inn offers nine guest rooms and four suites, each decorated with rich wallcoverings and fabrics, and furnished in original antiques. All have spacious private baths, armoires and queen-or king-sized beds; several have private decks, fireplaces and jacuzzi tubs. The Emerald Isle Room, with shamrocks and Lily of the Valley decor, is named in honor of Kathy's mother. Relax outside on a private deck or in the old-fashioned claw-foot tub. The jacuzzi tub in the Amadeus Room lends a splash of the contemporary to the room, whose elegant rose decor evokes Mozart's 18th century. In colors of burgundy, tan and red, the Concours d'Elegance reflects Dan's fondness of antique automobiles. A cast-iron stove warms the sitting room of this suite, which also features a claw-foot tub and plumbed wash stand. Original-stained glass windows throw a special light on the Dollie McKeen Suite, named for the woman who nurtured apartment-dwellers here from 1923 until her death in 1965. The room has hosted golden wedding anniversaries for two couples who had lived in the building during their college days, met and married. An antique fireplace, jacuzzi bath and shower add to the warmth of the suite.

Celebrations of Spirit

Each Thursday night, five blocks of Main Street are closed off to host the Farmers market, which Kathy says "is more like a community celebration, with cloggers dancing and bands playing". "There are puppet shows, and local restaurants barbecue on sidewalk grills", explains kathy. "It's been going on for 10 years, and is different every time." San Luis Obispo is also the home of the internationally acclaimed Mozart Festival, which is now in its 22nd year (it was on the way to a performance that Mozart joined the Smith family). The two-week festival, which begins in late July, features world-class professional performers.

Neighboring towns hold special surprises as well. Fifteen miles from San Luis Obispo is Morro Bay, a small fishing village where you can find a variety of ocean fish. Unique shops and art galleries line the

Guests can relax in the Goldtree library.

streets of nearby Cambria, one of our favorite small seaside towns. Just minutes away are Avila and Pismo beaches for swimming, surf fishing, surfing and relaxing in the sun. Ask Kathy or Dan for directions to the Hearst Castle. Built in 1920, this is the second most popular attraction in California. Also worth a visit are the 30 or more wineries that dot San Luis Obispo county, from famous labels to small family-run establishments. You'll also have an opportunity to sample many of these local wines during the wine and cheese hour at the inn.

Getting There

From Highway 101, take the Marsh Street Exit. Drive north on Marsh for six blocks, then turn right onto Chorro Street. Drive one block and turn right onto Pacific Street. Drive one block and turn right onto Garden Street. The inn is on the right side of the street with a burgundy awning.

THE MARTINE INN

Address: 255 Oceanview Blvd., Pacific Grove, CA 93950
Telephone: (408) 373-3388; toll free (800) 852-5588; FAX (408) 373-3896
Location: Facing the water on Monterey Bay.
Hosts: Don and Marion Martine, Tracy Harris
Room Rates: $115 to $225 double, includes breakfast
Credit Cards: MasterCard, Visa
Remarks: No pets. Smoking in fireplace rooms only.

The Martine Inn is a gracious bed and breakfast overlooking Monterey Bay. Built in 1899, the original home was true Victorian. It was owned for many years by the Parke family of Parke Davis Pharmaceuticals, who converted it to a Mediterranean-fashioned villa. The Martine family purchased the home in 1972, and Marion and Don fully renovated it in keeping with the Victorian traditions. "Everything we do helps to create an authentic turn-of-the-century environment, from our antique silver service to the recipes we use to prepare our food," says Marion. "Our goal is to treat our guests in the same gracious manner as they would of been treated if they had been guests of the Parke family during the early 1900s." And the mission has been successful; the Martine Inn was named one of the "Ten most romantic inns" by *Vacation Magazine*, and one of the "Twelve best inns in the United States" by *Country Inn Magazine*.

Complete Suites

In renovating the inn, the Martine's took particular care with details. Inlaid oak and mahogany floors were hand restored, and the wall coverings and paint carefully selected in keeping with the era. Each of the 19 rooms is individually decorated with elegant museum quality antiques. The Martine's have searched extensively for complete bedroom suites for each room and have unearthed some interesting finds. The Edith Head Room contains her own bedroom suite as well as a commissioned portrait; the McClatchy Suite is furnished from the estate of C.K. McClatchy; the Park Room features a 1860 Chippendale Revival four-poster bed, complete with canopy and side curtains. The Pewter Room lives up to its name down to the pewter light fixtures.

Ocean Views

Thirteen of the rooms have a wood-burning fireplace, for which wood is provided. Many have an ocean view, and all have private bath. Two oceanside parlor areas allow those without view rooms a

place to enjoy the water vista. An enclosed, landscaped courtyard offers a quiet spot for reading and is also an ideal site for weddings of 125 people or fewer. Parties of over 35 must reserve the entire inn for their special events. A conference room is available that will accommodate up to 20 for meetings. For fun and games, visit the game room with its 1890's billiard table and nickelodeon. The glass enclosed pool room and jacuzzi hot tub are located off the courtyard. Ask Don about his MG collection, and find out how he did recently racing one of his prized antique cars.

Elegant Service

The oceanside dining room contains an impressive collection of silver and china, all carefully selected by Don and Marion. A 1765 Old Sheffield server, Victorian condiment and pickle service, and signed Tiffany loving cups are but a few of the treasures to be found in the cupboards. A lovely Victorian-style china service is used for breakfast, and coffee is served in individual Victorian silver pots.

Our favorite time at the inn is in the evening, as twilight spreads across the California coast, guests of the inn gather for hors d'oeuvres and a glass of wine in the parlor. While a fire warms the room, guests sample an array of appetizers from puffed pastry filled with fresh vegetables and herb cream cheese, garnished with a rose petal, to delicious crab and cheese balls, and spanokopita. There is something magical about standing there enjoying good food and wine, while at the same time watching the sea otters enjoying their own social rituals in the kelp-beds just across the street.

Breakfast is a meal not to be missed. Ismael Vizcaya, the inn's long-time chef, prepares fresh and wonderful creations such as "Eggs Castroville", salmon Wellington or Monterey eggs and salsa. Fresh fruit, juice and homemade breads accompany the meal. Viscaya is also available to cater the many weddings, meetings and other functions held at the inn.

On The Peninsula

The Martine Inn enjoys a prime location on the Monterey Peninsula within easy walking distance of many attractions. The Monterey Aquarium is just four blocks and features nearly 100 innovative habitat galleries and exhibits. Monterey's historic Fisherman's Wharf houses a large fishing fleet, and has its share of shops and seafood restaurants. A walking tour of historic Monterey, called the Path of History, winds past the wharf on its lovely rose and herb garden-lined route. Our favorite walk in Pacific Grove is the Victorian tour, which takes you past homes of the 1800s, and The Pacific Grove Museum of Natural History is six blocks from the inn.

Dine while watching the sea otters at play.

The staff at the inn is dedicated to creating a pleasurable, well-rounded experience for the guest. They are able to arrange golf and tennis games, bike rentals, and suggest local dining establishments. The inn's library is stocked with literature on nearby attractions as well as menus from most restaurants.

Some of the finest sites of the Monterey Bay area may be seen from the comfort of the Martine Inn. Winter is the best time to watch for migrating whales and to curl up by the fire as the storms come in over the ocean. Otters and seals play in the surf year-round, and seabirds feed along the shore right in front of the door.

Getting There

From Highway 1, take the Pacific Grovel Pebble Beach turnoff. Follow signs on Highway 68 to Pacific Grove (the road becomes Forest Avenue). Stay in the right lane all the way to Ocean View Blvd. Take a right and proceed 15 blocks to the inn. Private parking is available in front of the Inn.

INN AT DEPOT HILL

Address:	250 Monterey Avenue, Capitola-by-the-Sea, CA 95010
Telephone:	(408) 462-3376; FAX (408) 458-0989
Location:	Four miles south of Santa Cruz off Highway 1
Hosts:	Suzie Lankes and Dan Floyd, Owners/Innkeepers
Room Rates:	$155 to $250 double
Credit Cards:	American Express, MasterCard, Visa
Remarks:	Two-night minimum over a Saturday night. No pets. Handicapped accessible. Smoking on outside patio area only. Full breakfast, afternoon tea or wine and hors d'oeuvres, after-dinner dessert and complimentary off-street parking.

For an exotic get away, try Paris or the Italian Riviera. But if your time is limited, visit the Inn at Depot Hill, two blocks from the sea in the city of Capitola on Monterey Bay. Designed in the grand style of the old-world, it's the next best thing to a romantic European escape.

In the main room you will first sense the history of this 1901 building, which was originally a depot for the Southern Pacific Railroad, connecting the Santa Clara Valley to the sunny shores of Capitola-by-the-Sea. This Corinthian-columned building welcomed thousands who alighted from the "Sun Tan Special," eager to enjoy a seaside retreat from the intense heat of the valley.

Authentic Furnishings

The parlor is lined with bookshelves to its 14-foot ceilings. An unusual round sofa may have held visitors awaiting their return home. A 1909 baby grand piano has been augmented with silicon chips to play a variety of music, and a fireplace warms this and the adjacent dining room, which once housed the depot's ticket windows. Two wing chairs and a table sit in front of a trompe l'oeil scene that creates the illusion of looking through a dining car window, complete with an ocean vista. Here, you will enjoy a full breakfast of fresh fruits from the local farmer's market, granola, fruit juices, croissants, cinnamon rolls and muffins. There is always a hot dish, from eggs benedict to delicious quiches. Take afternoon tea or wine and hot hors d'oeuvres onto the patio and relax among roses, azaleas and colorful trumpet vines that surround a reflecting pool and a herringboned brick patio and pergola. The courtyard is a perfect setting for small weddings and receptions, and the inn can provide all decorations, flowers and catering for the event.

Exotic Destinations

Co-owner Suzie Lankes attributes her interest in railroads to her grandfather who once worked as chief architect for Southern Pacific. Suzie explains, "I traced the journeys of railroads on the maps of Europe to the exotic destinations that lay at the tracks' end. We designed the rooms to reflect these beautiful, elegant places."

Each of the inn's eight rooms were decorated by San Francisco designer Linda Floyd. The Cote d'Azur has a lovely needlepoint rug on terra-cotta tile floors and a canopied iron bed. Faux painting on the room's columns lends the room a continental air. Portofino, in shades of green and camel with a hand-painted grape wreath above the marble fireplace, is fully handicapped accessible. The Paris Suite, in vivid black and white, is upholstered in French toile with windows covered in French lace. A fireplace opens to both bedroom and sitting area.

The pink and green floral draperies and striped sofa of the Sissinghurst English Garden Room reflect the beautiful gardens found there. From the canopied bed you can view the fireplace at eye-level. A pillow-filled windowseat is the highlight in the Stratford-on-Avon, which also has a verdigris iron table ideal for composing Petrarchan sonnets. The Delft Room is our favorite, with the soothing blue and white, from the delft tile surrounding the fireplace to the chaise. Its feather bed is covered in a white Belgium linen comforter and has floor to ceiling white linen bed drapes.

The Railroad Baron gives a taste of how railroad entrepreneurs must have lived. Overstuffed red velvet chairs provide a perfect spot for reading in the sitting area, which is separated from the bedroom by white columns with heavy draperies of gold silk. The focus of the skylighted bathroom is a two-person soaking tub. Capitola Beach is a contemporary environment of taupe and white. A beautiful checkerboard carpet and window seat with plump pillows encourage relaxation, and an oil painting of Capitola Beach and seashell sconces add finishing touches.

The books and paintings in each room reflect their themes, and each room is equipped with amenities to make your stay comfortable: concealed color television and VCR, in-room stereos, Egyptian cotton robes, hair dryers and coffee makers are just a few. All rooms have wood burning fireplaces and private marble bathrooms (many with double-headed showers). There is even a small TV in each bathroom. Ground-level suites have private patios and jacuzzis.

Dan Floyd, co-owner, says "people are truly surprised by the beauty of the rooms and by the personal service that we provide. Often people will make a reservation for their next visit as they check out!"

The Delft Room has a feather bed covered in white Belgium linen.

The inn is designed for the business traveler as well. Each room has a desk and phone equipped with FAX/modem connections. The entire inn can be reserved for business meetings. A choice of breakfasts and catered lunches and dinners encourage flexibility.

The engaging small-town atmosphere of Capitola offers art galleries, boutiques, sailing, fishing, swimming and surfing. Cyclists will enjoy the bike trails that wind through Big Basin National Park, and Pastiempo golf course is one of six area courses. Fifteen small wineries are nearby, each famous for their Pinot Noir, and adjoining Soquel is a center rich with treasures for antique lovers.

Getting There

From San Jose, travel south on Highway 17 to Santa Cruz, and south on Highway 1 for four miles to Capitola. Take the Park Avenue Exit and turn toward the ocean. Park dead-ends into Monterey Avenue. Turn left on Monterey and immediately left into the Depot's driveway.

THE BABBLING BROOK

Address: 1025 Laurel Street, Santa Cruz, 95060
Telephone: (408) 427-2437, toll free (800) 866-1131; FAX (408) 427-2457
Location: In quiet neighborhood
Host: Helen King
Room Rates: $85 to $135 double occupancy. Includes full country breakfast and afternoon wine and cheese.
Credit Cards: American Express, Carte Blanche, Discover, Master Card, Visa
Remarks: Children over 12 welcome. Handicap accessible rooms. No pets.

As you pull into the parking lot of this lovely Santa Cruz inn prepare yourself for the smell of Helen King's famous cookies as it wafts out the French doors and windows to greet you. Walking up the staircase that bridges the brook after which the inn was named, you'll begin to suspect that this is a place that will feel like home, and with the first smile from Helen, you'll know you were right.

"I try to have good smells coming from the kitchen all the time, whether it's from my cookies, breads, muffins or casseroles. When my six kids were in school, there was always some delicious smell waiting for them when they walked in the door. Now they look back on their childhood and whenever they smell baking cookies they remember Mom's kitchen; that's how I hope my guests will feel about the Babbling Brook."

A Historic Masterpiece

Beside the Babbling Brook's cascading waterfall lies an ancient protected Ohlone Indian burial ground. The property subsequently hosted an 18th-century grist mill run by Mission fathers and a tannery, complete with water wheel, during the Gold Rush days.

In 1924, Charles Chandler and his wife turned the property into a Roaring '20s retreat. Mrs. Chandler, had an upstairs built onto the existing log cabin, stone retaining walls, an enormous wine press, an outdoor stone bread oven and rotisserie, and elaborate gardens. Lloyd Wright bought the home in 1942 and used it as a restaurant, christening it "The Babbling Brook." The Babbling Brook Inn opened as the first bed and breakfast inn in Santa Cruz in 1981.

Garden of Earthly Delights

A small handcrafted sign on the inn's front deck reads "Time began

in a garden." That's easy to believe here. Standing on the redwood deck you hear the water of the brook and can scan the acre of redwoods and gardens that surround the inn. Surprisingly, you are actually situated in the heart of town, conveniently near the beach and the boardwalk, but secluded in the oasis provided by the grounds of the inn. Helen's most recent addition is an antique 14 foot, fully functioning water wheel.

The Babbling Brook offers 12 guest rooms- four are in the main house, and eight rooms are found in chalet-style cottages in the gardens. All of the rooms have private baths, and all but two offer woodburning fireplaces, and these feature Japanese deep soaking whirlpool tubs. Every guest room in the shingled cottages commands a romantic view of the hillside, overlooking gardens and brook. Rooms are individually decorated with the paintings and colors of a particular French Impressionist artist, and bouquets of freshly cut flowers complete the soothing atmosphere. This is a place to discover, or rediscover, romance.

The Honeymoon Suite has a large antique bathtub and canopied bed, with a private balcony where the waterfall and brook enter the grounds. The suite, like all of the rooms but one, has a private entrance. Most rooms have balconies with French doors that open onto decks. Helen has filled the rooms with special, "homey" touches, using the finest Laurel Ashley linens, and tucking them in with beautiful hand-woven Kennebunk throws. Don't worry, if you grow too attached to your blanket, Helen also has a few for sale.

The comfortable living room is filled with soft chairs and sofas. Here, you can sit by the fire playing backgammon or cards, listen to the soothing piano music in the background, or read through Helen's restaurant book, in which guests have written their reviews of more than 100 local restaurants.

Helen's Breakfast

Under a skylit atrium, charming breakfast tables await you, for a breakfast at Babbling Brook is no ordinary experience. Helen, whose cooking has won awards, presents a buffet of homemade croissants, a variety of breads, muffins, Helen's special orange almond granola, an egg dish and wonderful coffee and juices. A tea tray filled with her cookies sits in the foyer, and you'll seldom see it empty. When you return from an afternoon of boardwalk strolling or beach town browsing, wine and cheese are available to take the edge off hunger before you decide what to explore in the way of dinner.

The Babbling Brook is one of our favorite places to come and hideout. Helen is a gracious and attentive hostess, and a visit to the inn does indeed feel like a trip home—the serene surroundings and the sounds of the brook create a dramatic yet restful climate.

Romantic suites border the gardens and the brook.

An engaging Bohemian throwback to the surf cities of yesteryear, Santa Cruz maintains a refreshingly carefree air. Surfers peddle by with their boards. Early morning docks are lined with fishermen drinking strong coffee and predicting the day's forecast, as the music of the boardwalk's carousel swells to meet the day. Scenic jogging paths take you along the coastal cliffs.

Fall brings the migrating whales close to the coast and the sea lions to nearby Año Nuevo State Park. The Monarch butterflies come home to beautiful Natural Bridges Beach Park. The University of California at Santa Cruz's Shakespeare Festival is touted as one of the best.

Getting There

From the north, take Highway 17 to Highway 1, toward Half Moon Bay. Follow Highway 1 and turn south on Laurel Street at the signal. The inn will be a couple of blocks down on your right. From the south, take Highway 1 through town to Laurel Street. Turn left and proceed almost two blocks toward the ocean. The inn will be on your right.

INN AT UNION SQUARE

Address:	440 Post Street, San Francisco, CA 94102
Telephone:	(415) 397-3510; toll free (800) 288-4346
	FAX (415) 989-0529
Location:	One-half block west of Union Square
Host:	Brooks Bayly, General Manager
Room Rates:	Guest rooms $110 to $180, Suites $145 to $400
	(Penthouse); $15 per additional guest
Credit Cards:	American Express, Diners Club,JCB, MasterCard,
	Visa
Remarks:	Expanded Continental breakfast; afternoon tea;
	wine and hors d'oeuvres. Children welcome.
	Handicapped accessible. Fee for valet parking with
	in-out privileges. No smoking in hotel. Room ser-
	vice available for dinner. No pets.

In the heart of San Francisco's urban plaza is the Inn at Union Square, a personalized alternative to the city's large commercial hotels. This European-style, 30-room inn provides a service-oriented, calm respite for business travelers and tourists alike.

The building dates back to 1924 and has always served as a hotel. In 1980, noted interior designer Nan Rosenblatt and her husband Norman, transformed the old hotel into a quietly elegant, full-service inn. Their talent and attention to detail is exemplified in this charming hotel.

Personalized Attention

"There's a strong trend for travelers to move from large, impersonal chains to smaller hotels that provide a warm, friendly environment. For guests who do not wish to stand in lines, who enjoy being recognized by name, we're their kind of hotel," explains Norman.

The Inn at Union Square assures this degree of personalized service by building a team of people to attend to your needs 24 hours a day. No request is too large or too trivial, from making theater and restaurant reservations, to providing a complimentary shoe shine.

Each of the hotel's six floors contains a comfortable lobby with fresh flowers, a round table and wing chairs in front of a wood-burning fireplace. It's here, overlooking Post Street, that you may enjoy the expanded Continental breakfast. Set with china, napkins and placemats, the table is stocked with fresh fruit, juice, hot coffees and teas.

Hot muffins and flaky croissants are delivered upon your request; an assortment of cereals is also available.

From 4 p.m. to 6 p.m., the mood turns social for afternoon tea. An assortment of cookies, finger sandwiches, nuts and fruit accompany a variety of teas. Between 6 p.m. and 8 p.m., you may enjoy the complimentary wine and hors d'oeuvres while relaxing around the fire and getting to know fellow guests.

You may have any of these provisions delivered to your room, or choose a full-course dinner from a catalog of the city's finest restaurants. An honor bar and a large wine list are also available to complement your meal.

Elegant Rooms

The inn's mirrored hallways are lit by handsome brass wall sconces. Brass lion-headed door knockers open to each guest room. Accommodations range in size from twin bed arrangements to grand king-sized beds, and all rooms have full shower/tub combinations in their private baths. Sleeping areas are set away from the street to provide quiet and privacy. There are several room arrangements that accommodate families or parties traveling together.

A queen suite offers separate living room with fold-out love seat, chairs and a television. A two-bedroom suite provides ample space, and has a wet bar and a sitting area. The penthouse suite features a fireplace and wet bar in the separate living room, and a bedroom with a canopied bed and spacious walk-in closet, and a sauna with a whirlpool bath.

Each room is individually designed according to a traditional mood. Soft colors on the walls and fresh flowers on the mantle promote serenity. Flowered fabrics drape the bed, and are echoed in the draperies and half-canopies with mahogany headboards. Georgian antiques add warmth and beauty, while goosedown pillows assure a good night's rest.

We appreciate the special attention which has been given to the details. Side tables house pull-out writing shelves. Baths are papered in coordinated patterns and offer spacious shelves, hand-milled soaps, plush towels and terry robes. In the morning one of five newspapers will be delivered to your door.

The inn's location makes it very accessible for business travelers. The hotel, with an adjacent meeting facility, has the ability to handle conferences of 12 to 40 people and receptions for 60. Modem connections, secretarial services, FAX, copying, and a complimentary 800 number and credit card dialing provides additional comfort.

The rooms are all set back from the street for quiet sleeping.

San Francisco's Finest

The inn is ideally located to provide easy access to the interesting neighborhoods which made "The City" as wonderful a place to live as it is to visit.The city's famous shopping district, Union Square, is around the corner; the financial center is just 10 minutes away. The inn is surrounded by theaters and world-renowned restaurants. Public transportation, from cable cars to city sightseeing buses, connect you with Ghirardelli Square and Chinatown, Golden Gate Park and the countless other vistas the Bay has to offer.

Getting There

From the San Francisco Airport, take Highway 101 north to the Seventh Street Exit. Cross over Market Street, keeping in the right lanes. Turn right on Leavenworth and go seven blocks to Post Street. Turn right on Post Street and travel three and a half blocks and the inn is on the left side under the green awning.

WASHINGTON SQUARE INN

Address:	1660 Stockton Street, San Francisco, CA 94133
Telephone:	(415) 981-4220; toll free (800) 388-0220; FAX (415) 397-7242
Location:	One block from Telegraph Hill on San Francisco's Washington Square
Host:	Brooks Bayly
Room Rates:	Rooms $85 to $180; $10 per additional guest
Credit Cards:	American Express, Diners Club, Master Card, Visa
Remarks:	No smoking in hotel. Children accepted. No minimum stay required. No pets. Fee valet parking with in-out privileges. Complimentary Continental breakfast, afternoon tea, wine and hors d'oeuvres.

San Francisco history greets you as you step outside the mirrored doors of the Washington Square Inn. If you squint your eyes, you can almost see Lillie Hitchcock Coit straining to see the fire engines roar past. Across from the landmark cathedral of St. Peter and Paul, a memorial stands, which is Coit's gift "To commemorate the Volunteer Fire Department of San Francisco 1849-1866."

The sights and smells of the city waft by — focaccia baking, fresh coffee beans roasting, Coit Tower rising into the sky. The Inn at Washington Square offers a particularly authentic experience of old San Francisco.

This 15-room hotel is housed in a building dating back to 1908. In 1978 designer Nan Rosenblatt and husband, Norman, transformed it into one of the city's first specialty hotels. Since that time, the hotel has continued to cater to business travelers and people who enjoy being close to all that San Francisco has to offer.

Refined Comfort

Each of the inn's 15 rooms was decorated and furnished by Nan to reflect a feeling of quiet elegance. Florals mix with soothing greens, blues and peaches in draperies and bed covers. Half-canopies grace king and queen beds. Mahogany and brass headboards complement large armoires and antique tables. Original artwork is set off against painted walls. Each room holds freshly cut flowers.

Rooms are arranged to offer various combinations. One of the main floor rooms has a king bed with two sofa-beds, ideal for families. Two rooms overlook private courtyards filled with a profusion of

ferns and flowers. These rooms offer king beds, goosedown chair and sofa that opens to a twin bed. We particularly enjoyed the spectacular view of Coit Tower from a window seat of a double-bed room with half-bath. Two of the larger rooms offer luxurious window seats over bay windows, the perfect location for watching the activity in Washington Square.

Eleven of the rooms have separate baths with comfortable amenities. Terry cloth robes, thick, thirsty towels and hand-milled soaps refresh and restore a tired body. Four rooms share papered, roomy baths with shower-tub combinations. Halls are lit with brass chandeliers.

Visiting in The Parlor

One of our favorite gathering places is the inn's parlor, where guests congregate in the mornings and afternoons. A goosedown sofa and cushioned arm chairs in front of the antique-mantelled fireplace provide a comfortable place to sit and relax.

Continental breakfast, served around the handsome French dining table or brought on a tray to your room, consists of fresh fruits, juice, hot brewed coffee or tea, and an ample selection of baked goods. Afternoons offer a quiet time for wine and hors d'oeuvres of nut mixes, smoked salmon, pate, grape leaves and a variety of cheeses. Evenings bring turn-down service and if you'll leave your shoes outside your door, a complimentary shine. Valet service is also available.

Business traveler needs are fully met at the hotel. All rooms have telephones. A FAX machine is available for use, and secretarial services and other business meeting needs are filled at the inn's companion hotel, the Inn at Union Square.

Host Brooks Bayly described the style of the inn: "The level of service offered by the inn's staff captures what the hotel is designed to be - a place where guests always know that they can have as much privacy as they want combined with as much service as they need. We gain the most satisfaction when we receive a letter saying how much a guest enjoyed the hotel. That makes our job worthwhile."

Focus on Environmental Needs

When the hotel announced that it had enforced a no-smoking policy, its owners and staff were recognized by the American Cancer Society for their steps to provide a clean and healthy environment. As a further step, aerosol sprays are not used in hotel cleaning.

The inn is perfectly situated to help you discover and enjoy the parts of San Francisco which have charmed and delighted visitors for over 100 years. The inn is located amid the bustle of Columbus and

The comfortable rooms face the interesting North Beach neighborhood.

Stockton streets, a contrasting collection of all that an urban setting provides. In walking distance you can dine in a variety of old-style North Beach restaurants and coffee houses. Enjoy walking tours of Chinatown. You're also just a short distance from Fisherman's Wharf and Ghirardelli Square, or a short cable car ride from Union Square.

Getting There

From the San Francisco Airport go north on Hwy 101 toward the Bay Bridge. Exit at Fourth Street (last exit before bridge). Go straight one block on Bryant and then left on Third Street past Moscone Center. As you cross Market Street, Third becomes Kearny. Stay in the left lane and veer left on Columbus. At the three-way intersection at the top of the hill, turn right on Stockton. The inn is located on the corner of Stockton and Filbert. From the Golden Gate Bridge follow Highway 101 to Marina Exit. Follow Marina to Safeway, then turn right on Laguna and left on Bay street. Turn right on Stockton Street. The inn is located on the corner of Stockton and Filbert.

THE MANSION AT LAKEWOOD

Address: 1056 Hacienda Drive, Walnut Creek, CA 94598
Telephone: (510) 945-3600
Location: In the San Francisco bay area suburb of Walnut Creek
Hosts: Sharyn and Mike McCoy, Owners
Room Rates: $125 to $250 double. Includes generous continental breakfast.
Credit Cards: American Express, Discover, MasterCard, Visa
Remarks: No pets. No smoking.

For a retreat into remote rural elegance that's only minutes from urban adventure, pack your bags and make your way to The Mansion at Lakewood. This graceful country estate is set on three secluded acres of wooded property that feels like it's a million miles from any city. Host Sharyn McCoy assures you, however, "you can walk to Nordstrom or be on BART transit system to San Francisco for shopping in just five minutes." This is in the unlikely event that you'll wish to leave the mansion, whose special environment and attention lend credence to the concepts of chivalry, true love and, of course, to white rabbits.

Rebirth of an Elegant Country Estate

The Mansion at Lakewood has quite a story to tell. Originally part of a 2,000-acre Mexican land grant to the Pacheco family in 1834. In 1908, the developer of the now beautiful Lakewood area, Robert Noble Burgess, bought the property and, by adding expensive embellishments, transformed a farmhouse into a country manor for entertaining businessmen and friends in luxurious style.

The McCoys, residents of Walnut Creek, purchased the mansion and its three acres of lovely trees and flowers in 1987. After a year of careful renovation and planning, the newly restored masterpiece was opened to the public at Christmas 1988.

Through a 19th-Century Looking Glass

In a suburban city full of the impatience of the young, The Mansion at Lakewood clings to the elegance and dignity of a bygone era, paying the 20th century little mind. Through the mansion's gates lies a protective haven, one that provides respite to all who enter. Sharyn says many of her guests are local residents who come to enjoy the feeling of going away without really going away. And should you, in

the midst of your discoveries look up to find a respectable looking rabbit hiding beside the baseboards or under your bed, don't be alarmed. They, too, feel the magic of the mansion.

After ringing the original hand crank doorbell (stamped October 23, 1860) and stepping through, you'll be struck by the whimsy of Sharyn's assortment of inanimate rabbits that peek at you from inauspicious places. Mike's playful humor and Cheshire cat grin belie his career as a nuclear engineer. Sharyn's twinkly eyed presentation of freshly baked cookies and homemade lemonade is enough to make you think that you may be in Wonderland after all.

The manor's seven richly decorated guest rooms — all with private baths and distinctive appeal — are the product of Sharyn's imagination and creativity. The Attic Hideaway is tucked up against the stars, among piles of pillows and intimate nooks. In the Summerhouse you'll enjoy a feather bed, atrium bath, sunny porch and private entrance. The extraordinary raised platform antique brass bed in the coveted Estate Suite wraps you in damask and soft goose down. This suite also features a crackling fireplace, French doors that open onto a private terrace, and a gleaming black marble bath with sunken jacuzzi for two.

Sharyn's thoughtful touches are found throughout the house — fresh cut wildflowers, turned down bed service with chocolates and orchids, and the opportunity to indulge in the mansion's delicious (and prodigious!) continental breakfast at your leisure. "We really do focus on romance," Sharyn notes, "especially on the weekends." She places heart-shaped truffles on heart-shaped doilies on the table in each room. "We can arrange any kind of special evenings, including candlelight dinners, picnics on the lawn, an Engagement Package complete with limousine service, a private suite and a quiet dinner for two—we can generally accommodate any request."

The mansion's bright drawing room, parlor and majestic library, which has a glowing marble fireplace, can be reserved for small corporate retreats or intimate social gatherings. Business travelers find The Mansion at Lakewood to be a refreshing change of pace, and the proximity of the BART transit system into San Francisco makes the mansion as convenient as it is comfortable. "We have more people sitting in front of the fire with their laptop computers these days," laughs Sharyn.

The expansive ground and gardens provide the perfect site for a romantic, old-fashioned wedding, amidst century-old oaks, magnolias, eucalyptus, redwoods and an assortment of wildflowers. Sharyn can arrange weddings of up to 60 people around the sun-filled gazebo on the lawn, or beneath the mansion's ancient hickory tree. In the morning, a Victorian love poem is delivered to the newlyweds' room with breakfast.

The seven guest rooms are all richly decorated.

Walnut Creek is only 25 miles from the heart of San Francisco. The Mansion at Lakewood provides guests with easy access to a host of Bay Area activities. The Regional Center for the Arts has produced such an outstanding selection of plays, music, symphonies and cultural events that the United States Conference of Mayors declared Walnut Creek the most liveable city for its size in the nation. Add to that the John Muir Museum, the annual Walnut Festival, the hiking, horseback and hang gliding at nearby Mt. Diablo State Park, and you'll agree that The Mansion at Lakewood provides the perfect location for whatever you want to do, wherever you want to go.

Getting There

From San Francisco, cross the Bay Bridge and take Highway 24 toward Walnut Creek to the Ygnacio Valley Road Exit. Follow Ygnacio Valley Road approximately one mile to Homestead. Turn right on Homestead and pass one stop sign. The next left is Hacienda. Turn left on Hacienda to the white wrought iron entry gates of The Mansion. Push the gate call box on the left to notify of your arrival.

WINE & ROSES COUNTRY INN

Address: 2505 W. Turner Road, Lodi, CA 95242
Telephone: (209) 334-6988
Location: 35 miles south of Sacramento
Hosts: Kris Cromwell, Del & Sherri Smith,
                   Owners/Innkeepers
Room Rates: $79 weekdays; $99 weekends; $69 corporate week-
                   day rate
Credit Cards: American Express, MasterCard, Visa
Remarks: Children welcome. Handicapped accessible.
                   Complimentary wine upon arrival. Full country
                   breakfast.

Authentic country inns are hard to come by in the West. The Wine & Roses Country Inn is an outstanding example, combining elegant lodging with exquisite food. When Lodi's well-known, grape-growing Towne estate was sold by its owners, Kris Cromwell, her son Del Smith and daughter-in-law, Sherri Smith saw the possibilities to create a wonderful country inn..

Through their artistry and hard work, they refined the 90-year-old farmhouse into a fashionable 10 room country inn. Its clapboard exterior got a fresh coat of white paint. Its guest rooms were transformed with rich floral prints, deep-hued walls, hand-made comforters and antiques. The inn is secluded on three acres of towering trees and old-fashioned gardens.The lush, green lawn is as comfortable for a game of croquet as it is for a wedding party.

Chef Sherri Smith, schooled at the Culinary Academy in San Francisco, has developed an outstanding French country restaurant. Dishes are complimented with a fine hand and with fresh flowers from the garden. The dining room is intimate-rose walls and carpeting, with lace curtains, Victorian chandeliers, piano and fireplace. Tables are set with fine china, linens and at each place setting, the inn's signature, a fresh rose.

Start the meal with a chilled prawn cocktail or a warmed wedge of brie topped with carmelized apples and crackers. Entrees include several classically prepared pasta dishes, Madeira-sauced veal cutlets, and an array of fresh seafood with fresh fettucini. Grilled loin lamb chops are marinated in rosemary and garlic and served with a minted fruit sauce. All entrees are served with home-baked bread, soup or salad, and fresh garden vegetables. Desserts range from chocolate decadence cake to a puff pastry filled with fresh strawberries and cream.

Country Charms

Each of the inn's guest rooms is individual in nature, all named after songs. From Garden Party, which features an old-fashioned claw-footed tub in the center of the room, to Carousel, a fantasy of carousel horses and brass bed. Guests enjoy a glass of wine or soft drink upon arrival. In the morning Sherri serves a full gourmet breakfast featuring the "Country Inn Scramble," a puff pastry filled with scrambled egg, cream cheese and smoked turkey.

Business travelers find the inn equipped with televisions, phones, and clock radios, xerox, FAX and computer capabilities. For the exercise-hungry, the inn can schedule a game of tennis, golf or a workout at the nearby health club. An early Continental breakfast is offered on weekdays to fit busy schedules.

Getting There

From Interstate 5, south of Sacramento or north of Stockton, take Turner Road Exit and drive east 5 miles. The inn is on the left. From Highway 99, take Turner Road Exit and drive 2.5 miles, the inn is on the right.

This is one of California's few country inns.

AMBER HOUSE

Address:	1315 22nd Street, Sacramento, CA 95816
Telephone:	(916) 444-8085; toll free (800) 755-6526; FAX (916) 447-1548
Location:	Eight blocks east of the capitol
Hosts:	Jane Ramey and Michael Richardson
Room Rates:	$80 to $115; deluxe rooms with jacuzzi $145 to $195
Credit cards:	American Express, Diner's Club,Discover, MasterCard, Visa
Remarks:	No smoking. No pets.

As you enter the turn-of-the-century room that bears his name, you can imagine Henry Wadsworth Longfellow, ensconced in his Cambridge study. The 1905 Craftsman style, brown-shingled Amber House is a refuge for modern-day poets and business people alike. Its bevelled glass front door and wide porch sporting the American flag welcome you to an elegant retreat near the center of the city.

The main parlor reflects a marked attention to detail - an old rubbed brass chandelier, oil paintings, and antique victrola. The bookcase-lined library is a perfect spot for morning coffee or a meeting. The dining room features stained-glass windows that replicate the leaded glass in its built-in hutches.

Time to Read a Book of Poetry

The five guest rooms in the main house are all named for poets. Longfellow's Room has a queen bed, a romantic bathroom with an antique porcelain tub beneath a skylight. Lord Byron is warmed by camel walls with an iron and brass queen bed, and jacuzzi in the bath. Emily Dickinson's Room features a double iron bed and detached private bath with shower and pedestal sink. Each is provided with phone, clock radio, cassette player and cable television.

Adjoining the main house is the Artist's Retreat, a 1913 Mediterranean that houses a parlor/meeting room, dining room, and three luxurious guest rooms. Rooms are designed in colors and fabrics to reflect the vibrant artists for which they are named. Renoir is an elegant mini-suite with king half-canopy bed, sofa and antiques. The full-canopied queen bed in Degas is washed in pinks and mauves. In Van Gogh's green and white marble tiled solarium bath a waterfall flows into the lighted, heart-shaped jacuzzi for two.

These rooms are furnished with antique armoires holding a color television, VCR, and radio/cassette player. Each suite features separate phone lines with call waiting, forwarding and conference calling. The inn charges no fees for local or credit card calls.

Guests Needs Come First

We particularly appreciated the special touches such as pre-breakfast coffee or tea delivered to your door. There's a little jar of cookies to munch on in each room. Wine and champagne (or mineral water) are always ready. Jane and Michael make sure that the inn offers the highest quality amenities. Personalized service ranges from help with daily activities and dinner reservations to serving a full breakfast, in the dining room or in individual rooms, at a time set by the guest.

Just eight blocks from the capitol, the inn is situated at the hub of the city. The state capitol and its surrounding grounds offer a rich walking tour. The heritage of this historically rich area is centered in Old Sacramento, 28 acres of Gold Rush-era buildings.

Getting There

From San Francisco take Interstate 80 east. In Sacramento, stay on Business 80. Take the 15th Street Exit. The Inn is eight blocks east of the capitol between Capitol and N streets.

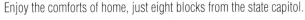
Enjoy the comforts of home, just eight blocks from the state capitol.

THE BEAZLEY HOUSE

Address: 1910 First Street, Napa, CA. 94559
Telephone: (707) 257-1649
Location: The southern end of the Napa Valley
Hosts: Jim and Carol Beazley, Owners and Innkeepers
Room Rates: $125 to $180, including full breakfast
Credit Cards: Master Card, Discover, Visa
Remarks: Two-night minimum on weekends. No smoking.
                  Carriage House is handicapped accessible.
                  No pets.

When Dr. Adolph Kahn built his home in 1902, he expected to house only his family and a private medical practice. Ninety years later, this Napa landmark lodges guests from around the world, eager to relax in its elegant turn-of-the century atmosphere.

Jim and Carol Beazley have restored this colonial revival style home, which sits on a quiet tree-lined street. Set against brown shingles, blue and white striped awnings shade five bay windows. The stained-glass door on the wide, pillared front porch opens onto a foyer filled with botanical prints, oriental rugs and an old wagon filled with teddy bears.

Comfortable sofas and chairs in the living room invite relaxing by the fire, or you may want to hang around in the sitting area, playing a game. A steaming cup of tea in the afternoon is the perfect accompaniment to Carol's famous chocolate chip cookies, delivered to you hot out of the oven, unless you snatch one from the kitchen, which is my usual trick.

The Beazleys have paid careful attention to authenticating the decor of the inn. The music room, once the scene of afternoon concerts, holds music stands and cello. It also houses a large selection of classical music that fills the house throughout the day and evening.

Napa's First B&B

When Jim and Carol purchased the mansion over 11 years ago, the Beazley House became Napa's first bed and breakfast establishment. The Beazleys are the managing innkeepers and are involved with guests, property and staff

Their outgoing personalities and varied backgrounds suit their roles as innkeepers. Jim worked for 10 years as a photo journalist. His photographs hang throughout the inn. Carol worked as a nurse for 17 years. When they decided to change their careers and buy an inn,

they researched for two years before finding the perfect place for them and their children. They've never regretted the move.

Their interest in and enthusiasm for their work are apparent. "There's something in a good innkeeper that wants to nurture people, to help them enjoy themselves," said Jim. "And there's an attention to detail, to service, really caring for people. It's a very personal business. And that's why we love what we do."

Victorian Rooms

Six of the inn's most authentic rooms are located upstairs. Complete with period furnishings, chairs, brass lamps and armoires, all of the rooms have brass or Victorian queen-sized beds with floral spreads, soft pillows and carefully papered walls. Each room has a private tub and/or shower bath. The Sun Room, with dark floral patterns on white wicker, has a large bathroom with a 6-foot claw-footed soaking tub. The Master Bedroom has its own fireplace, whose flames are reflected in the room's gold decor. The soft pinks and blues of the Wedgewood Room echo the colors in the flower garden just outside the window.

The Carriage House, across the gardens from the mansion, is the "country side" of the Beazley House. In this two-story, brown-shingled building are the largest and most private suites. Each room has its own fireplace and two-person spa, as well as a queen-or king-sized bed. All rooms have separate entrances, and in some cases, a private garden. The Bed of Roses has a spa right in the room. The West Loft is framed by a beautiful stained-glass window of grapes and vines, and the crackling fire under an open beam ceiling creates quite a romantic atmosphere.

Each morning a full buffet-style breakfast is served in the dark paneled formal dining room. Typical fare includes Carol's freshly baked pineapple bread or muffins, a hot crustless quiche or potato dish, fresh fruit and yogurt. There's always granola as well as orange juice and Beazley blend coffee, ground fresh for each pot. Over breakfast, the Beazleys offer suggestions of activities and will gladly make reservations for meals and special events.

Business Travelers

The fully air conditioned Beazley House is particularly well suited for the mid-week business traveler. The inn is equipped with FAX, copier and a dedicated phone line for modems.

The Beazleys can also fill special orders. Flowers can be ordered and ready for your arrival, and wine may be chosen from an extensive wine list for delivery to your room.

All the rooms have brass or Victorian queen-sized beds.

Napa is a primary hub of the many activities available in the valley. A walking tour of Old Town explores a variety of period architectural styles. Wild Horse Valley offers hiking trails and lots of open space, and there's beautiful scenery to enjoy while biking through Skyline Park. Take an opportunity to explore some of the smaller wineries in the southern Caneros region of the valley. The cool growing climate there is best suited for the finest in Chardonnay and Pinot Noir wines.

Getting There

From San Francisco, drive over the Golden Gate Bridge. Go North on Highway 101 to Highway 37, following the signs to Napa/Sonoma. Go East on 37 to Highway 121/12 marked Sonoma/Napa. At Highway 29 turn left (north) , go the the Central Napa/ First Street Exit. Drive 3/10ths miles to Warren Street. Turn left on Warren, to First Street. The inn occupies the northwest corner of Warren and First.

NAPA VALLEY BALLOONS

Address:	P.O. Box 2860, Yountville, CA 94599
Telephone:	(707) 253-2224; toll free in California (800) 253-2224
Location:	Napa Valley wine country
Host:	Don Surplus
Rates:	$165 per person
Credit Cards:	American Express, Discover, MasterCard, Visa
Remarks:	Reservations required.

Napa Valley is a valley for all seasons. In the spring, corridors of mustard plants radiate vibrant golden hues, brilliantly lit against the dark wild oaks. In summer, the fields are a quilt of earthy wheat browns and grapevine greens. In autumn, the vine's leaves are transformed into a patchwork of colors as rich as the grapes they bear. Amidst the groves of eucalyptus and pine, between the stands of ancient oaks, rest grand chateau wineries.

There is no better way to experience Napa Valley than via a hot air balloon ride. The 26-mile long valley is known for its gentle, predictable winds. Most days are ideal for flying, especially in the fall and winter. Napa Valley Balloons, Inc. is well equipped to create a safe and memorable experience. Established in 1978 with the launching of a single balloon, the company has expanded their fleet to 14. Eight pilots and a large supportive ground crew comprise the competent staff. It is the largest company in the valley, carrying about 8,000 passengers annually.

Dawn Over Napa Valley

The Napa Valley ballooning experience begins at dawn, before the sun's warmth causes the winds to kick up. Balloons are launched from various sites in the valley, but often they leave from the Domaine Chandon Winery. We joined in the excitement of helping hold open the balloon as its gaping mouth was shot with flame. This is a great time for photos as the balloon begins to rise like a giant awakening from a nap. The wicker gondola is then boarded by up to six passengers and a pilot, and the colorful, inverted pear balloon lifts gently from the earth.

Climbing to around 1,000 feet, the balloons ride the air currents, gracefully maneuvering through the valley. The elevation is altered by the degree of heat blasted into the balloon. The pilots scan the vista, assessing the winds, continually changing the balloon's altitude to steer by the currents. One moment you are skimming along just above the grape vines, then steadily soaring to view heights. We were both surprised at how much we could see of the valley which we have totally missed during years of driving the roads.Having never been up in the air without a motor nearby, the quiet was eerie at first but soon we adjusted and could hear sounds from miles away.

After a flight of about 45 minutes, you will spot the chase crew driving below, following the balloon as the landing spot is picked. Following the balloon flight, a champagne celebration takes place. A table spread with elaborate trays of cheeses, cold cuts, fresh bread, baskets of fruits, vegetables and dips awaits. Champagne and orange juice flow freely as the successful flight is toasted. Staff members join in the fun, snapping souvenir photos for participants, singing songs and ceremoniously presenting a balloon replica pin.

Ballooning is a safe sport, and the staff have flown with small babies and centenarians alike, and all land with a certain effervescent smile and a special memory of their lofty experience.The only thing you really need to bring is a camera.   Always reconfirm your departure time and location the night before, although the final launch decision is not made until sunrise.

Getting There

Yountville is on Highway 29 north of Napa. Directions to the specific meeting spot will be given upon confirmation of your reservation.

This is the best way to see the Napa Valley.

THE WINE COUNTRY INN

Address: 1152 Lodi Lane, Saint Helena, CA 94574
Telephone: (707) 963-7077; Fax (707) 963-9018
Location: In the middle of the Napa Valley wine growing region.
Hosts: Jim Smith, Innkeeper and Diane Horkheimer, Manager
Room Rates: $125 to $175 double; $20 per additional guest. Rates include Continental breakfast.
Credit Cards: American Express, MasterCard, Visa
Remarks: No pets. Children discouraged.

The Wine Country Inn sits among the cultivated vineyards of Napa Valley, a part of California's famous wine producing region. Just as fine vintage wines are wrought of total dedication and love, so is this family operated country inn.

Family Ties

One of the oldest continually operated inns in the region, The Wine Country Inn began as Ned and Marge Smith's dream. Intent on opening an inn, they traveled extensively on the East Coast to gather ideas. They wanted to recreate the look and character of older inns, yet add the comforts available today. The Smiths engaged the entire family in the creation of their inn. The men did the masonry, building and furniture refinishing; the women stitched the quilts, comforters and pillow slips. Their efforts resulted in a three-story stone and wood structure that blends beautifully with the vintage wineries it neighbors.

Country Views

Because of the inn's placement on a knoll, almost every room offers a country view. Wild mustard, lupines and poppies flourish, and a row of Chinese pistachios line the driveway. Each of the inn's 24 rooms has a character trait setting it apart from the others. Private balconies, large patios edging the lawn, snug window alcoves, a hand-painted canopy bed, or a Victorian headboard reworked to handle a queen-sized mattress all await your discovery. Fifteen of the rooms have a free-standing fireplace. All rooms have a private bathroom and air conditioning while some have piped in classical music with individual volume control. The antique furnishings are from various periods; each has been selected by the Smiths.

Quiet Nooks

What each of the rooms has in common is comfort. There are no televisions or radios, yet there are plenty of books and quiet reading nooks. There are pastoral views and intimate rooms ideal for romance. The inn has an outdoor swimming pool with plenty of lounge chairs around it, and a large bubbling spa nearby. Pool towels and robes are provided.

Nearly Continental Breakfast

The inn's Common Room is the gathering place for a hearty Continental breakfast served daily from 7:30 a.m. to 9:30 a.m. Homemade granola, a variety of breads from zucchini to banana, fresh juice, fruits and coffee comprise the morning meal. Guests can eat around the large refectory table or outside on the deck. The Common Room is also well stocked with books and games to keep you entertained during other times of the day. Pots of tea water and coffee steam continually. A refrigerator is available for guests' use.

The Wine Country Inn is not far from over a dozen fine restaurants that serve lunch and dinner. Their menus are stacked on a Common Room table for guests to review, and the staff will be glad to make the phone call to secure a reservation. Now that's hospitality.

The Wine Country

Napa Valley is the largest and most popular of the wine regions in the state. Between the cities of Napa and Calistoga, over 215 wineries dot the valley. Their volume ranges from 500-case cottage wineries to million-case producers. The valley can be quite crowded during the summer weekends. We suggest planning a visit during the less hectic months between October and April. Another hint for enjoying your visit is to venture forth during the morning hours, then retire to the pool at the inn during the warmer midday. Then, as the others start to leave, you dry off and start enjoying the wineries again. Among the valley's old and great wineries are Beringer, Christian Brothers and Charles Krug. Sterling Vineyards, accessible by tram, sits like a monastery on a knoll over the upper valley.

Most wineries in the valley are open to the public and offer tours and tasting; a few wineries may be visited by appointment only. The Wine Country Inn staff will provide information on wineries and wine tasting and make appointments for guests as requested.

St. Helena, the wine country's capital, is noted for its 40 wineries and historic buildings. Chic shops, restaurants and scenic parks line the main street through town. The Silverado Museum features

All the rooms come with pastoral views and intimate settings.

Robert Louis Stevenson memorabilia, where over 7,000 items recount his life and global adventures.

Calistoga, Yountville and St. Helena are artist communities, where galleries are filled with local paintings, crafts and photographs.One of the best ways to view the wine country is via an early morning hot air balloon ride. Bicycling is popular in the valley, and hiking is enjoyed in the surrounding hills. Several places offer horse rides into the surrounding hills, a great wat to have a picnic.

Getting There

From San Francisco, take the Oakland Bay Bridge, Highway 80, then head northward to Vallejo. Travel west on Highway 37 and turn right on Highway 29 north through St. Helena.Two miles past the down-town , turn right on Lodi Lane. Go east one-quarter mile to the inn, which will be on your left.

SILVER ROSE INN

Address: 351 Rosedale Road, Calistoga, CA 94515
Telephone: (707) 942-9581
Location: One mile east of Calistoga in the Napa Valley
Hosts: J-Paul and Sally Dumont
Room Rates: $110 to $160 Sunday through Thursday; $125 to $185 weekends and holidays
Credit Cards: Discover, MasterCard, Visa
Remarks: Complimentary breakfast and afternoon crackers and cheese with bottle of Chardonnay. Two-night minimum stay on weekends. No children or pets.

A lifetime interest in good foods and good wines made J-Paul and Sally Dumont steady visitors to the Napa Valley. They would visit the valley often to add new varieties of wines to their personal collection. On one of their trips in 1985, they happened to visit the Silver Rose. They immediately fell in love with the property and its potential, the vineyards and pastoral land that rim the property.

"In our travels we have stayed in numerous inns. We designed the Silver Rose to reflect what we enjoyed most — an elegant but comfortable inn, and a place to sit back and relax," says Sally. At the Silver Rose, there are no televisions or telephones in the rooms.

The Silver Rose Inn sits on 24 acres of rolling hillside on the northern end of the Napa Valley, just one mile from the town of Calistoga. The sheep grazing in the fields as you come up the drive affirm the peaceful atmosphere that reigns over the wood-framed ranch style inn. A silver rose, the signature of the inn, is etched into the stained-glass on the front door and on the labels of their exclusive Silver Rose Cellars Chardonnay.

J-Paul and Sally greet you as if you've come home for a family visit. A crackling fire in the lava stone fireplace warms the expansive, two-story gathering room. Under a redwood-beamed ceiling are large, comfortable easy chairs and sofa, perfect for enjoying the room's plentiful supply of books, magazines and games. Tile floors set off rich Oriental rugs and tables are accented with colorful linens.

Through the floor-to-ceiling window you can see the blue umbrellas near the outdoor swimming pool and jacuzzi. The carefully designed rock garden is offset by a gentle waterfall that feeds the pool. Reading-in-the-shade options are provided by a redwood bench under a 300 year-old oak, and in the rose-encircled gazebo.

Those same roses turn up on your breakfast table, along with a delicious array of fruits, many fresh from the garden, and speciality breads. Sally bakes all her own bread and muffins, many based on recipes handed down from her Scottish grandmother. As breakfast is served there is plenty of piping-hot house-blend coffee, tea and fresh orange juice to start off your day. If a guest prefers privacy, breakfast can be brought to the room and enjoyed where views of mountains, vineyards and pastures of grazing sheep and lambs can be savored. On chilly mornings, there is always a fire in the large stone fireplace in the gathering room. This provides a warm and relaxing place to enjoy the morning meal and visit with the other guests. We have found taking breakfast around the pool, near the waterfall to be a wonderful way to start the day.

The five guest rooms are decorated according to a specific theme, and open onto the gathering room. All have private baths, and several feature a private balcony. A profusion of teddy bears inhabit the whimsical Bears in Burgundy Room, while Victorian elegance pervades the Turn-of-the-Century Room. The Oriental Suite has beautiful hardwood floors, shoji screens and a private jacuzzi. All of the rooms have queen-sized beds, tables and comfortable chairs.

You may want to work out in the gym, which is fully equipped with universal equipment and free weights, or enjoy a snack of crackers and assorted cheese to accompany your bottle of Chardonnay.

Extraordinary Engagements

The warm atmosphere of the Silver Rose makes it ideal for accommodating small groups. The entire inn may be reserved for business meetings, anniversary parties, reunions or small wedding parties. On these occasions, J-Paul and Sally exercise their local authority to arrange unusual activities for their guests.

Sharing an already infectious passion for food and wine, the Dumonts arrange blind and vertical wine tastings at the inn, and at selected wineries throughout the region. They can also set up barrel tastings and dinner parties in the winery caves. In the summer, you can enjoy a barbecue or a special picnic on the patio, or plan a black tie dinner, catered by the finest restaurants in the area, to be served in the formal dining room.

"When guests leave the Silver Rose, we hope they will have enjoyed the tranquility of the valley, and perhaps, learned a little more about its fine wines." J-Paul adds, "We hope they will have had the opportunity to experience some of our special places, away from the busy hustle of life."

People from around the world come to visit the hundreds of wineries in the Napa Valley, which holds a diverse assortment of activities

The inn is an ideal setting for private parties.

ranging from rigorous to relaxing. We are more inclined to explore the valley during the morning hours, then retire to poolside for the afternoon. We are then ready for more activity during the late afternoon as most visitors are starting to leave. Neighboring Calistoga has long been renowned for the comfort and respite provided by its natural hot mineral waters and soothing mud baths. Glider planes and hot air balloons offer an eagle's perspective of the valley below. Bicycles can be delivered right to your door for a leisurely ride through scenic country lanes, and the historic Sharpstein Museum provides an authentic look at the early days of the wine country and life in the 19th century.

Getting There

From San Francisco, take the Bay Bridge, then follow Interstate 80 to Highway 37. Drive west on Highway 37 to Highway 29 and north to Calistoga. Travel through town, turn right on Silverado Trail to Rosedale (One mile). Turn left on Rosedale, then right into drive.

BELLE DE JOUR INN

Address: 16276 Healdsburg Avenue, Healdsburg, CA 95448
Telephone: (707) 431-9777; FAX (707) 431-7412
Location: 70 miles north of San Francisco
Hosts: Tom and Brenda Hearn, Owner/Innkeepers
Room Rates: $115 to $165 Suites
Credit cards: Master card, Visa
Remarks: Rates include full country breakfast. Two-night minimum on weekends. No smoking. No pets.

When Tom and Brenda Hearn found themselves talking by car phone while stranded in traffic jams on separate Los Angeles freeways, they knew it was time for a change. Within five months, the Hearn's became the new owners of Belle de Jour.

Driving into this pastoral country setting, one understands the reasons why they would choose such an environment. Roads and wineries in the heart of this wine-producing valley are less crowded and more scenic than what many city dwellers expect.

Belle de Jour's setting on six rolling acres is uncluttered and relaxing. An old red barn sits on the property and hammocks hang from the olive trees. A well used wine vat has found new life as a "cold tub" on the redwood deck.

Individual Cottages

Tom and Brenda designed the inn to reflect the amenities they most enjoy— individual cottages that provide privacy and relaxation. "Guests have an opportunity here to feel at ease, to be alone, to choose when and if they wish to socialize," said Brenda.

Battenberg lace canopy and comforter bedeck the shaker pencil post king bed in the Caretaker's Suite. Antique English and American pine mix with crisp, white wicker. Rough-hewn walls that once enclosed a grain and tack room are transformed into a natural, refreshing space. The bathroom is a delight, with makeup mirror and lights, and teal blue-tiled whirlpool tub for two.

From the forest-green whirlpool tub in the Terrace Room, you view rolling pastures and private patio. Soft florals cover the brass king bed. The airy feeling of Atelier is enhanced by Ralph Lauren florals and rag rugs. A suspended canopy from the vaulted ceiling envelopes the queen bed. Rattan sofa and chairs in its sitting area front the blue-enameled Vermont castings woodstove. The tub and shower have jacuzzi jets.

Adirondack chairs on the lawn outside The Morning Hill Room overlook trees and rolling pastures. Furnished with antiques and a woodburning stove, this suite has a lace-curtained bay window and large armoire in the foyer. Florals in soft greens and pinks cover french doors and queen English cottage bed. The shower and steam bath holds two people. Suites are furnished with fresh flowers, ceiling fans, air conditioning, refrigerators, hair dryers and sun-dried sheets.

A full country breakfast is served every morning. Guests sit around the French farmhouse harvest table to enjoy fresh fruit, hot muffins and croissants, freshly brewed coffee, tea and juice, and hot entrees like crab quiche or eggs Benedict. If you prefer, a basket, with china and crystal, can be delivered to your room.

For a special day, have Tom give you his customized back road and winery tours in his 1923 Star open touring car.

GETTING THERE

Follow Hwy 101 north to Healdsburg. Take the Dry Creek Road Exit. Go right at bottom of ramp and go a quarter mile to the second light. Turn left on Healdsburg Avenue. The entrance to the inn is across from Simi Winery Tasting Room.

The romantic suites are nestled on six private acres.

WHALE WATCH INN BY THE SEA

Address: 35100 Highway 1, Anchor Bay, CA 95445
Telephone: (707) 884-3667; toll free (800) Whale 4 - 2
Location: On the Mendocino coast
Hosts: Joanna Wuelfing, Innkeeper; Jim and Kazuko
                         Popplewell, Proprietors
Room Rates: $160 to $250 double; Includes full breakfast
                         served in your room.
Credit Cards: American Express, MasterCard, Visa
Remarks: Two-night minimum on weekends. Three-night
                         minimum on holiday weekends. Not suitable for
                         children. No pets. Smoking permitted on decks.

Perched on the edge of the Mendocino coast, 90 feet above Anchor Bay near the little town of Gualala, the Whale Watch Inn has been described as "about as close to perfect as you can get." We know from our travels that when we seek a quiet, restful and romantic retreat, we head for the Whale Watch Inn. Everything about this inn, from its cliff top location, the expansive ocean views, the sound and smell of the surf below and the efficient staff, all work to provide guests with a memorable experience.

Suite Selection

Each of the 18 guest rooms offers dramatic views of the coast and the ocean beyond. The inn was built in stages from 1974 through 1985 and now consists of five buildings on a meticulously land-scaped setting. The tasteful touches of Jim and Kazuko Popplewell are everywhere. All the rooms have queen-sized beds covered with lacework linens and thick, down comforters. Soft shades of pastels and vaulted ceilings with skylights enhance the mood of each room's interior. The fireplaces add to the romantic setting. Most rooms have another sure-to-please amenity - large two-person spas with whirlpools. Private decks are ideally suited for sipping wine and watching the moonlight dance on the surf below.

The Bath Suite, our perennial favorite, features a spiral staircase leading to a second story whirlpool bath with a skylight and a 270-degree view of the coast. Four suites in the Sea Bounty building offer fully equipped kitchens, making them ideal for longer stays. All rooms offer private entrances and decks.

The original building houses two small guest rooms and a large common room featuring floor-to-ceiling windows and an expansive deck. The Whale Watch Room also has a fine library, with emphasis

on natural history and marine life books, an assortment of games and puzzles, and a telescope for scanning the Pacific. Sofas and easy chairs make it the perfect place to curl up with a good book or reflect on the spectacular view. Wine and cheese are served around the fire on Saturday evenings. With no television or telephones, the atmosphere offers the utmost in peace and relaxation.

Breakfast In Bed

Jim and Kazuko and their staff go to extra effort to make certain that your day starts off well. Breakfast is prepared and delivered to your room. Most guests like to have it served to them while still in bed. The hearty early risers can also have it served while out on their private deck. Kazuko says, "We want to make breakfast at the Whale Watch really special for our guests." In addition to the staple items of fresh-brewed coffee and tea, fresh seasonal fruits, juices and home-baked breads, guests will find Belgian waffles, mushroom crusted quiche, or crepes filled with fresh fruit in a cream sauce.

Coastal Beauty

Guests are free to wander through the gardens that comprise much of the two-acre site. A large grassy knoll with an incomparable view of the ocean is a highly acclaimed site for outdoor weddings.

At the edge of the bluff, a private stairway leads to the secluded beach 90 feet below. Beach walking and tidepool exploring are year-round events. From December to April, migrating California gray whales are frequently sited.

Tennis, golf and horseback riding are not far away, and six miles south of the inn along Highway 1 is Gualala Point Regional Area, where hiking trails ramble along bluffs and headlands. Beach access and picnic facilities are available.

The charming town of Gualala has a number of art, craft and photography galleries.This historic community has a colorful past; Pomo Indians, Russian trappers, Mexican landowners, German settlers and Chinese cooks have all had a hand in settling the area. At the Sea Ranch, just five miles south, is a nine-hole golf course that has been honored as one of the best in the United States. A selection of restaurants is within a short drive of Gualala. The inn staff is well acquainted with the area and happy to assist in making reservations.

Point Arena Lighthouse,15 miles north of Gualala along Highway 1, stands on the point of the U.S. mainland closest to Hawaii. The area is site of countless shipwrecks. First constructed in 1870, the lighthouse stood until 1906 when the lens and tower were destroyed by the great San Francisco earthquake. The rebuilt tower has withstood

The Whale Watch Room overlooks Anchor Bay.

the rigors of nature to this day. A museum at the base tells the story, and a tour includes a trip to the top.

Highway 128 runs eastward from the coast into the heart of the Anderson Valley and some of Mendocino's premium wineries, where you have a chance to sample wines and even meet the wine makers. The staff can plan an itinerary for you including arranging for some winery tours.

Getting There

Take Highway 101 north to the Central Petaluma/Bodega Bay Exit. Go west through Two Rock and Valley Ford to Bodega Bay. Follow Highway 1 north to the Whale Watch Inn at Anchor Bay, five miles north of Gualala. Or, take Highway 101 to the River Road turnoff, four miles north of Santa Rosa. Go west through Guerneville to Jenner. Follow Highway 1 north to the inn.

THE STANFORD INN BY THE SEA

Address:	P.O. Box 487, Mendocino, CA 95460
Telephone:	(707) 937-5615; toll free (800) 331-8884; FAX (707) 937-0305
Location:	At Coast Highway 1 and Comptche-Ukiah Road in Mendocino
Hosts:	Joan and Jeff Stanford, Owners/ Innkeepers
Room Rates:	$160 to $250; includes champagne breakfast.
Credit Cards:	American Express, Diners Club, Discover, MasterCard, Visa
Remarks:	Two-night minimum on weekends. Pets accepted.

The century-old town of Mendocino perches on a broad headland of northern California's rugged coast. Once a thriving logging community, Mendocino's Victorian buildings are now home to art galleries, handicraft shops and fine boutiques. Mendocino is one of those rare travel finds that needs to be slowly savored. There is no better way to appreciate the Mendocino area than by staying a few days at The Stanford Inn by the Sea.

Innkeepers Joan and Jeff Stanford bought the property in 1980, and since that time, have dedicated themselves to building what Jeff calls "a truly unique, healthy place—a place for 're-creation'." Joan adds, "The inn provides an opportunity for people to get excited about life again." Walking through the gardens, visiting the inn's llamas and horses, canoeing, sitting on a rock by the ocean, lounging on their deck or in front of their fireplaces, "often people will experience something really nice in themselves, learn something new, just by taking some time to unwind."

Country Charm

Each of the inn's 23 rooms opens onto a deck, offering panoramic views of the ocean and the grounds. Each has a private bathroom stocked with fragrant soaps. Wood-burning fireplaces add country-fashioned warmth. The rooms are tastefully decorated with country floral prints, sleigh or four poster queen- and king-sized beds, authentic antiques, fine reproductions, and natural wood paneling. Plants and books create a home-like atmosphere, while a bottle of local vintage wine on a silver platter adds a pampering touch.

A small Nantucket-style cottage near the river contains two lovely suites, each equipped with full kitchen, separate bedroom and a living room. The Stanford amenities, including wood-burning fireplaces, grace the suites, which overlook the inn's canoe livery.

After a restful sleep, guests wander into the cheery lobby to assemble their breakfast trays. Under a copper domed server are warm

croissants or pastries. Freshly squeezed orange and grapefruit juice, a baskets of fruits, sliced melon and citrus, coffee or tea, yogurt, granola, cereals and chilled champagne complete the meal.

After breakfast, you may linger in the lobby, take a walk through the gardens, watch the llamas graze or black swans swim, or pick up the daily paper for a leisurely morning on your flower festooned deck, or perhaps pool-side in the newly finished greenhouse.

The recent addition of the new greenhouse-enclosed swimming pool, spa and sauna is a delight. Under a translucent ceiling is a tropical environment featuring orchids, fishtail palms and bougainvilla surrounding the 24-foot by 41-foot pool. A visit here is more than a physical workout; it is a sensual seduction. The fragrant plants, the classical music, the thoughtful decor invite the senses to open and receive. It is a very special experience to come from a day of brisk activities and then have this greenhouse pool available for a total change in mood.

Big River Nurseries

A California-certified organic garden, Big River Nurseries, produces lettuce, herbs, spices, onions, garlics and other vegetables for local restaurants and mail order, using French intensive, biodynamic and organic growing methods. Some of the nursery's "raised beds" also provide roses and other varieties of flowers. The garden's herbs and dried flower wreaths are found throughout the inn. Jeff and Joan believe that the gardens are intrinsic to the "re-creative" experience of the inn, and gladly share them with their guests.

Catch-A-Canoe and Bicycles Too!

The Big River winds through a forested canyon that opens into Mendocino Bay. Its undeveloped shores are home to a host of wildlife, including deer, black bear, beaver and great blue heron. The first eight miles of the river are gentle tidal waters, ideal for canoeing and kayaking.

The inn owns and operates a canoe rental program called Catch-a-Canoe and Bicycles Too! Its fleet of high-performance canoes and kayaks are available for excursions on this Class I river. After a brief lesson, you can paddle into the wilderness for exploration, photography, fun and relaxation. We find the fall a perfect time to picnic upriver. The Stanfords also provide top of the line mountain and road bicycles for guest rental. You can take a ride along national bicycle route Highway 1, or explore off-road terrain where old logging trails weave through forests of redwoods and firs.

The comfortable well appointed rooms face the ocean.

Coastal Wanderings

The northern California coast offers intriguing sights in any season. The windswept shore is often battered by winter storms, which bring in driftwood, shells and other treasures. A long, beautiful beach is near the lodge, offering prime exploring, picnicking and sunbathing.

Strolling along Mendocino's boardwalk, one discovers nearly 75 galleries and shops. Decent restaurants are found in the town and along the coast, and the staff at the inn is very helpful in directing guests to the better finds. Van Damme State Park, also near the inn, has interesting pygmy forests.

Getting There

From Highway 1, head east on the Comptche-Ukiah Road, just south of Mendocino. The inn is clearly marked on your left.

THE GINGERBREAD MANSION

Address:	400 Berding Street, Ferndale, CA 95536
Telephone:	(707) 786-4000
Location:	Northern California, five west of Highway 101
Host:	Ken Torbert
Room Rates:	$105 to $135 double; suites $135 to $175. Off-season rates available November 1 to April 30. Rates include breakfast.
Credit Cards:	MasterCard, Visa
Remarks:	Two-night minimum stay on weekends and holidays. All rooms have private baths with showers. Smoking permitted on outside veranda only. No pets. Not suitable for children under 10.

The entire town of Ferndale has been declared a state historic landmark. It is in this town, one of the country's best-preserved Victorian villages, that you'll find the Gingerbread Mansion. A beacon of warmth and hospitality, this brightly painted bed and breakfast is set just off Ferndale's Main Street. The 19th century turreted structure evokes a world of enchantment and serenity.

The Victorian structures of Ferndale were nicknamed "Butterfat Palaces" by the Portuguese and Scandinavian dairymen who settled the area in the late 1800s. The ornate houses are still maintained by descendants of the "Cream City's" founding fathers. With no parking meters or stop-lights, Ferndale is a perfect place to spend a weekend, especially with the Gingerbread Mansion as your base.

A blend of Queen Anne and Eastlake architecture with intricately detailed "gingerbreading," the Gingerbread Mansion was built in 1899 for a local physician, Dr. H. J. Ring. He turned it into the Ferndale General Hospital in the 1920s. In search of an alternative to his city lifestyle, Ken Torbert bought the mansion in 1981, where he created an elegant romantic retreat.

"His and Her" Bubble Baths

Ken's meticulous care is evident in all nine guest rooms, which are large and individually decorated with antiques, stained-glass windows, period art pieces and comfortable, firm queen beds. Bathrobes are tucked in the dresser drawers, and hand-dipped chocolates are left by the bedside as the staff turns down your bed. Four rooms have wonderful old-fashioned, claw-footed bathtubs. Two of the suites feature a pair of these unique tubs.

Bountiful Breakfast

In the morning, a tray of coffee or tea waits on the hall sideboard if you'd like to take it back to your room. But it won't be long before enticing aromas lead you into the elegant dining room for breakfast. The two tables are beautifully set with Ken's rare collection of green Depression glass that is embossed with tiny ballerinas. Classic paintings of romanticized women hang on the walls.

A generous, European-style breakfast includes fresh fruits, juices, hardboiled eggs, two kinds of locally made cheeses (salmon cheddar and caraway jack), and a variety of homemade breads, muffins and cakes. As you polish off the last few crumbs, Ken prepares you for a day of exploring with a wealth of anecdotes from Ferndale's history and its colorful cast of characters.

Many Extras

Four parlors offer opportunity to relax and enjoy. Two, with fireplaces, are stocked with an excellent collection of books and games. In the afternoon, we have enjoyed the opportunity to gather with other guests to enjoy tea and a variety of cakes around the fire. The fourth parlor invites guests to participate in the completion of one of two 1,000-piece jigsaw puzzles of the mansion. No radios, televisions or telephones can be found in the mansion's optimally serene environment. (A parlor guest phone is available.)

For a more active visit, a fleet of one-speed bicycles (painted to match the house) is available. The garden outside is filled with extraordinary fountains, statuary and flowering plants. This lovely English garden and the mansion are often photographed professionally for magazines, calendars and books.

Things To Do

Ferndale is a town of artisans and "real" people who take pride in their town. There is an abundance of interesting shops, art galleries and museums. You may even drop in on an antique show . The highly acclaimed repertory theater hosts seven productions a year. The "Foggy Bottoms Milk Run" and the "Bicycle Tour of the Unknown Coast" are two local sporting events. Memorial Day boasts the classic "World Champion Arcata-to-Ferndale Cross-Country Kinetic Sculpture Race" a three-day affair where hundreds of entrants coax artistically welded contraptions toward the finish line. In June, the Mid-Summer Scandinavian Festival takes over Main Street. At Christmas, Ferndale decorates America's tallest living Christmas trees, a 125-foot Sitka spruce.

Each romantic room in individually decorated.

State and National redwood parks are north and south of town. Nearby Russ Park has miles of wilderness trails to explore. A long, untamed walking beach is just five miles from Main Street.There is a very special driving loop from Ferndale out to the Lost Coast (the most unexplored region of the California coastline). The loop continues over the mountains and comes back to Highway 101 through the redwood forests.

Getting There

The Gingerbread Mansion is located 260 miles north of San Francisco, and about 15 miles south of Eureka. Take the Fernbridge/Ferndale Exit off Highway 101. Follow the Ferndale-Victorian Village sign to Main Street (about five miles). Turn left at the Bank of America. Go one block to Berding Street. The mansion is on the corner.

CARTER HOUSE AND HOTEL CARTER

Address: Carter House, 1033 3rd Street, Eureka, CA 95501
                  Hotel Carter, 301 L Street, Eureka, CA 95501
Telephone: (707) 445-1390 (Carter House); (707) 444-8062
                  (Hotel Carter)
Location: In "Old Town" section of Eureka
Hosts: Mark and Christi Carter
Room Rates: $95 to $250 double; includes full breakfast at
                  Carter House or a Continental breakfast at Hotel
                  Carter
Credit Cards: American Express, MasterCard, Visa
Remarks: Complimentary wine and hors d'oeuvres served
                  from 6 p.m. to 7 p.m. in Carter House parlor and
                  the lobby of Hotel Carter. No pets.

Mark Carter, a native Eurekan with a penchant for Samuel and Joseph C. Newsom designs (architects of the local Carson Mansion, recognized as the finest example of Victorian architecture in the United States), scratched an itch when he came across plans by the same architects for a smaller Victorian. The plans detailed the 1884 mansion that stood in the middle of San Francisco until the great earthquake and fire of 1906. The Carter House was inspired by these old Newsom drawings of the destroyed house.

This romantic bed and breakfast inn opened in 1982 to rave reviews. The attention to detail in the big redwood home is impressive. The lavish detailing in the seven guest rooms is complemented by the simple interior design. Crisp white walls, polished oak floors spread with Oriental carpets, splashes of modern art all add to the bright, uncluttered feel of the rooms. Cozy down comforters and flannel robes are part of the ambience. Four rooms have private baths; three others share a light, spacious bath down the hall.

Guests staying at the Carter House have spread the news about the superb breakfasts. A typical morning might start with specially roasted coffee, freshly squeezed orange juice in a crystal glass, poached pear in caramel sauce, followed by a fruit muffin and a poached egg Benedict.

New Challenges

Always ready for new challenges, Mark built Hotel Carter in 1986 to provide comfortable accommodations for Eureka's business travelers and those seeking the benefits of a classic hotel. The Hotel Carter is a spacious 20-room establishment that also houses an innovative

restaurant. Reflecting the personality of its creator, it blends a contemporary California style with the old-fashioned values an Italian mother teaches her son when strangers come to call - greet them with open arms, offer a warm fire, a glass of wine and a houseful of laughter. Such is the hospitality you will find whenever you stay with Mark and Christi Carter.

The peach and ivory lobby of the Hotel Carter is enhanced by an eclectic display of contemporary art and bleached pine antiques. All rooms have private baths (some with jacuzzis), telephones and televisions. Several rooms have fireplaces. In the summer of 1992, an attic wine cellar, meeting room and four large guest rooms will be completed on the hotel's third floor. Each guest room will be equipped with a jacuzzi and fireplace.

Mark's latest addition to the Carter quarters is the Bell House. The three rooms in this Victorian cottage may be rented as a unit or as individual accommodations. Each room has a private bath, done in white marble, with a whirlpool tub; two have fireplaces. A complete kitchen and a living room with television, VCR, stereo, and video and CD libraries comprise the common space in the house. Valet service is also available to all of the Carters' guests.

Experience in Dining

In "the smallest space you've ever seen" Christi Carter and her team of chefs produce innovative meals with style and creativity. "Everything is bought and prepared the same day," says Mark, "because we don't have space for a commercial freezer." The hotel offers a four-course dinner service three nights a week. With "fresh" as the key ingredient, the menu features regional delicacies including North Coast seafood and a bounty of garden herbs and vegetables, many of which Mark and Christi grow themselves.

The appetizer might be squash cakes with créme fraîche or baked chevre with garden greens. You may find grilled duck breast with Zinfandel-blueberry sauce, pork tenderloin with chutney and homemade applesauce among the choice of entrées. Fresh seafood such as salmon, halibut, cod or scallops sautéed in garlic, lemon and fresh herbs, and a special vegetarian creation round out the flavorful selection. To finish off the meal, choose from a variety of pastries and desserts that Christi's crew prepares daily from scratch.

A Cultural and Recreational Cornucopia

The clean ocean air and smell of old traditions invites a tour through Eureka's Old Town. Explore the boutiques and antique shops or take a Victorian home tour in a horse-drawn carriage. You are likely to

Cozy down comforters cover the beds.

find some of the sights associated with a working seaport as well as finding contemporary establishments. There are three repertory theaters that offer year-round performances, and multitudes of festivals like the annual Rhododendron Festival, the Blackberry and Octoberfest Festivals, which celebrate the area's ethnic and natural color. The grandeur of the North Coast wilderness is best illustrated by the Avenue of the Giants, just south of Eureka, and the "Lost Coast" offers unlimited pristine beauty for those seeking solitude. Humboldt Bay Cruises and the Arcata Marsh Sanctuary provide appreciation of the area's diverse marine and wildlife.

Getting There

From the north, follow Highway 101 into town (it becomes 4th Street) to L Street. Turn right. Go one block. From the south, follow Highway 101 through town. It turns right onto 5th Street. Follow 5th Street 13 blocks to L Street. Turn left. Go two blocks.

Pacific
Northwest

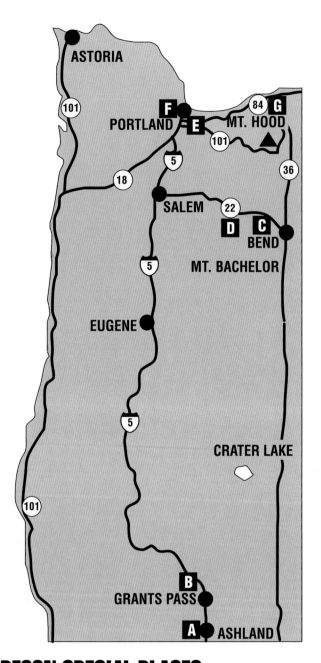

OREGON SPECIAL PLACES

A Romeo Inn

B Paradise Ranch

C Rock Springs Guest Ranch

D Black Butte Ranch

E Genoa Restaurant

F Heathman Hotel

G Columbia Gorge Hotel

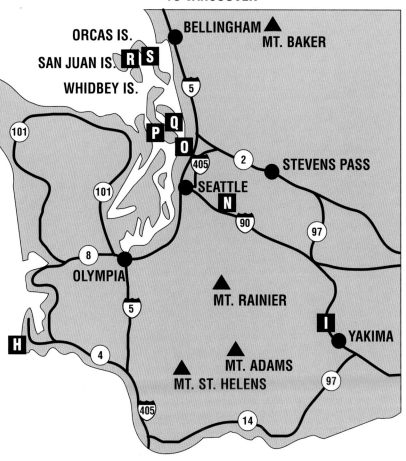

WASHINGTON SPECIAL PLACES

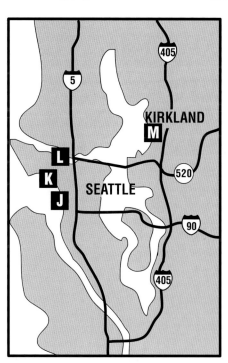

ROMEO INN

Address: 295 Idaho Street, Ashland, OR 97520
Telephone: (503) 488-0884; FAX (503) 488-0817
Location: In Southern Oregon near the California border
Hosts: Margaret and Bruce Halverson
Room Rates: $105 to $165 double
Credit Cards: Personal checks, MasterCard, Visa
Remarks: Two-night minimum stay June through September and on weekends from March through October. Children 12 and over welcome. No smoking and no pets.

Just as 17th century England was marked by Shakespeare's prolific genius, so has 20th century Ashland been transformed by its internationally renowned Oregon Shakespeare Festival. Whether you're in town to catch a performance of Richard III, or simply searching out a romantic refuge, you'll find what you need at the Romeo Inn. And more. The elegant Cape Cod style inn was built in the early 1930s and is set in a quiet residential neighborhood just eight blocks from the festival's center stage.

Margaret and Bruce Halverson purchased the inn in 1985 and created a place that guests have said "...feels just like home." "No, better than home." "This is a place where people can relax by the fire in the living room and breathe easily," explains Margaret. And they do, over and over again. At least half of the guests at the inn are repeat visitors, and many lasting friendships have been forged on the Halversons' back patio and around the library's baby grand piano. The inn's relaxing atmosphere is also ideal for small conferences of up to 20 people.

Rooms For What You Will

Accommodations at the inn consist of four spacious guest rooms and two deluxe suites. Each of the rooms have telephones, king-sized beds and private baths, with traditional and antique furnishings. Beds are covered with hand-stitched Amish quilts, custom-made for the Halversons. In addition to a lovely collection of fine art, Margaret's intricate needlework hangs throughout the house, adding to the personal environment of the inn.

The Coventry Room is upstairs and looks out over the flower gardens to the mountains. Also upstairs is the cheery blue and white Bristol Room, which offers a view of the pines and the valley beyond. The two downstairs rooms have private entrances, which

also accommodate guests with limited mobility, and daybeds for reading or lounging. Distinctive Oriental rugs warm the Windsor Room, and the Canterbury Room features a hand-crafted four-poster bed and a floor-to-ceiling brick fireplace.

The Cambridge Suite has a comfortable sitting area under a vaulted ceiling, where you can look out onto the pool and garden. The over-stuffed chairs are ideal for curling up before the tiled fireplace. French doors open onto a private patio with a view of the Cascade Mountains. Set apart from the inn for complete privacy is the Stratford Suite. With a full kitchen and living room, this suite offers a sweeping view of the Cascades, the Rogue Valley and the gardens of the inn. The marble fireplace provides warmth, as does the two-person whirlpool tub with a skylight view.

Love's Labor

Breakfast at the Romeo Inn encourages early rising, as the smell of apricot almond scones winds its way under the door to your room. A fresh fruit dish, such as a baked pear with minted walnut sauce, starts the meal off right. Margaret's award-winning yeast breads, including her famous lemon-cheese braid, accompany fresh-squeezed juices and coffee or tea. New entrees are developed each year. Scrambled eggs with sherried mushrooms and Belgian waffles with fresh blackberries and whipped cream are two favorites. Breakfast is served on one of the Halversons' five sets of fine china and includes bacon, sausage, ham or potatoes.To keep things inter-esting for returning guests, Bruce and Margaret maintain records of every individual's meals, and they try not to serve the same meals as previously enjoyed.

A Rose is a Rose

After breakfast, we suggest you follow our normal pattern and relax in the jacuzzi, enjoy a swim in the pool or explore the inn's gardens, personally designed by Bruce and Margaret. "The garden is com-pletely accessible for wheelchairs," says Bruce, "we've built special nooks so our guests can find a little bit of privacy if they want it." Here, over 600 varieties of flowers range through the year from spring crocuses and pansies, to daffodils and tulips. Bleeding hearts and sweet William brighten summer months. A pine-strung ham-mock and two garden benches encourage relaxation among the flowered grounds, and a fountain entitled "First Love" completes the English garden atmosphere.

Ashland has hosted the Oregon Shakespeare Festival since 1935. From March through October, the festival presents the work of

The pool is surrounded by gardens and the inn.

Shakespeare and many other playwrights, with as many as nine plays running concurrently. The town's theatrical offerings also include productions by Studio X, The Oregon Cabaret Theatre and the Actor's Theatre Company. The Rogue Valley Symphony, Opera, and The Oregon Ballet also perform regularly in Ashland. The Britt Festival in Jacksonville features jazz, dance, bluegrass and classical music under summer stars.

Getting There

From the south on Interstate 5, take Exit 11 (Siskiyou Blvd.) to Sherman Street. Turn left on Sherman, proceed two blocks to Iowa and turn right. Drive one block to Idaho, turn left and drive one block to the inn at the corner of Idaho and Holly. From the north, take Exit 19 to N. Main (Highway 99). Turn left on 99 and drive through downtown to Gresham. Turn right, drive four blocks to Iowa and turn left. Proceed one block and turn right onto Idaho.

PARADISE RANCH INN

Address:	7000-D Monument Drive, Grants Pass, OR 97526
Telephone:	(503) 479-4333
Location:	Near the Rogue River in southern Oregon
Hosts:	Jan Farr, Manager
Room Rates:	$78 to $125
Credit Cards:	Discover, MasterCard, Visa
Remarks:	Honeymoon and winter packages available at special rates. Pets and children welcome. Full service catering for weddings, parties and retreats.

The Rogue River carves a broad valley through southern Oregon, pausing in Grants Pass before making its final 50-mile journey to the Pacific Ocean. Sheltered by the Coast and Siskiyou Mountains, the valley enjoys a moderate, dry climate year-round. This is the home of Paradise Ranch Inn, probably one of the most stately little manors you'll ever run across. Located in the valley floor on 310 acres lined in white fences and dotted with black swans, it provides an excellent base from which to enjoy this scenic region.

Country Estate

The ranch, itself, resembles a gentleman's country estate. It was, in fact, a homestead cattle ranch when it was built in 1913. Three types of lodging accommodations are currently available to guests. The white clapboard stable-like building contains 13 guest rooms, six of which face onto a man-made pond. Country American decor prevails throughout. Rooms are furnished with queen- sized beds, and each spacious bathroom features a double-headed tiled shower. In keeping with the tranquil atmosphere of the inn, no televisions or phones are in the rooms.

The Gardeners Cottage is ideal for families with children. Equipped with a small kitchen, the Cottage will sleep up to four people, and is central to all ranch facilities. The Sunset House is set apart from the inn, offering total seclusion for families or couples. Equipped with a full kitchen, it sleeps up to eight in four bedrooms, each with king-sized beds and private bath. A wood burning stove and hot tub are among the home's amenities.

The recreation barn houses a grand piano, big screen television, pool and ping-pong tables, and a lounge area where guests can gather infront of the huge fireplace and enjoy a glass of wine before dinner. The facility is also available for business meetings, parties and wedding groups of up to 125 people.

Dining in Paradise

The Paradise Ranch Inn features two separate dining rooms, both with views of lovely ponds. In the distance, the many layers of the Coast Range are highlighted by the setting sun. The dining room is presided over by one of southern Oregon's finest chefs, who produces excellent cuisine based on seasonally available foods. Homegrown vegetables and herbs are used, as well as fresh local meats and seafoods. Rack of lamb, salmon, stuffed chicken with blueberry sauce and pasta dishes are favorite dinner entrees. A complete wine list features selections from Oregon as well as several imports. Fresh-ground coffee is a perfect accompaniment to the tempting array of desserts, from chocolate torte to fresh fruit pies.

The guests are served the Paradise continental breakfast to start the day off with fresh homemade goods. Also available by special arrangement is a large hearty ranch breakfast, enough to keep you full and satisfied for hours. We usually order a box lunch on the day we leave the ranch. Their good food helps improve any car trip.

Outdoor Fun

Two lighted tennis courts on the grounds are available to guests. The swimming pool is the place to cool off after a game of tennis, and the hot tub swirls away lingering aches. The ponds are stocked with largemouth bass and row boats are ready on the shore for an evening spin. A small island in the pond is equipped with a barbeque and a gazebo. It is an ideal spot for weddings and other special occasions. The inn has mountain bikes available for guests' use, and maintains a couple of miles of trails for walking or riding. A three-hole triangular pitch-and-putt course provides family fun.

The 1990s will see the completion of a new 18-hole golf course at Paradise Ranch Inn, as well as increased lodging and restaurant capacity. In addition to all the comfort and facilities you expect of a destination resort, the future of the ranch includes the development of private building sites.

Diverse Offerings

The Rogue River Valley offers a diversity of attractions, not the least of which is the Rogue River, itself. Grants Pass is the headquarters for several licensed guides who offer fishing excursions on the river. One- to four-day trips are available on kayaks, rafts, drift boats and paddle boats. A two-hour jet boat departs Grants Pass for 250-foot deep Hellgate Canyon. For landlubbers, a paved road winds along the Rogue northwest of Grants Pass, and hiking trails weave into the wild river section where no cars are allowed. Rogue fishing for sturgeon, steelhead and salmon peaks during winter, spring and fall.

The ranch has several ponds on the 310 acres.

The charming town of Ashland, nestled in the green foothills of the Siskiyous, is just south of Grants Pass along Interstate 5. Ashland is known for its excellent Shakespearean theater, the festival which lasts from late February through October.

Jacksonville, just 20 minutes from Ashland, conducts the Britt classical bluegrass, jazz, dance and musical theater festivals from late June through September first in the beautiful Peter Britt gardens. Be certain to take a good picnic dinner and a blanket to sit on, for these wonderful evenings under the stars.

Getting There

From southbound Interstate 5, take the Hugo Exit (Exit 66) and turn right onto Monument Drive. Proceed four miles to the Paradise Ranch Inn, on your right. From northbound Interstate 5, proceed to the Merlin Exit (Exit 61), north of Grants Pass. Turn left at the stop sign, then right onto Monument Drive. The inn is two miles down the road on the left.

ROCK SPRINGS GUEST RANCH

Address:	64201 Tyler Road, Bend, OR 97701
Telephone:	(503) 382-1957, toll free (800) 225-DUDE
Location:	Nine miles north of Bend
Hosts:	John and Eva Gill
Room Rates:	$1,350 per adult-single, $1,150 per adult-double, $875 per child 6-16, $675 per child 3-5. Saturday to Saturday. Open late June through Labor Day. American plan. Holiday rates available Memorial Day weekend, Thanksgiving and Christmas.
Credit Cards:	American Express, Diners Club, MasterCard, Visa
Remarks:	Baby-sitters housed and fed for small charge when traveling with family. No pets.

Nestled among the ponderosa pine and juniper forests in the foothills of central Oregon's Cascade mountains, Rock Springs Guest Ranch is a comfortable, unpretentious resort where guests quickly get to know each other and become part of an extended family. It is a place with strong traditions and ties. In fact, over half of the guests return each year.

Donna Gill, the dynamic founder of the ranch, is a bit of a legend in this part of the country. Listed among the Great Women of Oregon, Donna was one of the pioneers of the recreational industry. She built Rock Springs Guest Ranch with families in mind, and ran the ranch until she passed away less than a decade ago . Her nephew, John, and his wife, Eva, now continue the family tradition—the dedication to service for which Rock Springs is famous.

Catering to Families

Rock Springs Guest Ranch caters to families. Youngsters band together each morning with the youth counselors and enjoy a well developed program that includes horseback riding, evening hayrides, lunch rides, organized talent shows, hikes, swimming and an overnight camp-out. While children are off exploring, learning the mysteries of the outdoors and tales of the Old West, parents have a chance to spend a little time together. In the evening the kids meet again for more adventures, while the adults gather for hors d'oeuvres and conversation. Families with children under two who require one-to-one supervision are invited to bring along their own baby-sitter. The ranch will provide sleeping accommodations and meals for a minimal charge.

Eleven cozy, modern cabins sit among the tall ponderosa pines. These duplex, triplex and quad units feature cathedral ceilings and

knotty pine walls and accommodate from two to nine per cabin. All have private decks, and most have a fireplace, wet bar and sitting area; wood is stacked outside the door. The cabins are all newly remodeled; new carpet, furniture and linens help create a warm and inviting environment.

Rock Springs Guest Ranch operates on an American plan from the end of June until Labor Day. The week's package, which runs from Saturday to Saturday, includes lodging, all meals, horseback riding, youth program and lots of special activities. A modified American plan is offered for the holidays (Memorial Day, Thanksgiving and Christmas), which includes breakfast and dinner.

Prime Riding

The ranch keeps about 60 horses for its guests. John's sister,Leslie (she's a veterinarian), attends to the care and fitness of the riding stock. Rides go out in groups of six or seven people of similar ability to explore the adjoining Deschutes National Forest. Set against the backdrop of the magnificent snow-covered peaks of the Three Sisters, these are some of the best trails in the country.

In addition to horseback riding, there is a swimming pool, two lighted professional tennis courts, a sand volleyball court, horseshoes, croquet, fishing in the pond (stocked with bass and trout) and the option of doing nothing at all. The ranch also makes a good base for day trips to attractions in and around the Bend area. Among the favorites are Oregon High Desert Museum, Mount Bachelor for sightseeing, fly-fishing in top-rated Deschutes River and the spectacular scenery of Cove Palisades State Park. Spend a day with the Indians on the Warm Springs Reservation and Lava Lands Visitors Center. Newberry Crater and the volcanic country lie to the south of Bend, and there are also 13 golf courses nearby.

At the end of the day, when activity slows and muscles grow tired, relax in the ranch's custom outdoor spa. Set into a cave-like shelter of boulders, this is, perhaps, the most romantic setting we have ever found for a hot tub.

Well-Fed Guests

Rock Springs Ranch is well known for its delicious buffet menus. Breakfasts may include omelettes, homemade sticky buns, French toast, pancakes, waffles, fresh fruit, yogurt, granola, fresh coffee and juices. Ham, sausage or bacon and eggs also satisfy hearty morning appetites. For lunch you can expect one hot dish, plus sandwiches, soup, salad and cookies. Dinner ranges from fresh Northwest seafood to Mexican cuisine or perhaps prime rib. You have a choice of two entrées, vegetable, salad, fresh bread and dessert.

Comfortable, modern cabins are set among the tall ponderosa pines.

A Refreshing Environment For Gatherings

From September through June, the ranch turns its efforts toward corporate business meetings. Rock Springs provides a 4,400-square-foot conference center, equipment, lodgings and food service. Phones, FAXes and modems are also available. The ranch accommodates only one group of 20 to 50 people at a time. Groups may also take advantage of Rock Springs' forested setting for leadership and team-building exercises during their stay.

Getting There

To reach Rock Springs Ranch, follow U.S. 20 north from Bend for six miles to Tumalo. Turn west on the Tumalo Reservoir Road for three miles to the ranch. If you arrive by air, the Bend-Redmond Airport is 13 miles from Rock Springs. Rental cars and limo service are available, or arrange for transportation with the ranch.

BLACK BUTTE RANCH

Address: P.O. Box 8000, Black Butte Ranch, OR 97759
Telephone: (503) 595-6211; toll free (800) 452-7455 reservations; FAX (503) 595-2077
Location: On U.S. Highway 20, eight miles west of Sisters, in the Cascade Mountains
Host: Carrie Larsen
Room Rates: $80 standard room, $100 deluxe room, $130 to $170 one- to three-bedroom condo apartments, $100 to $210 two- to four-bedroom homes.
Credit Cards: American Express, Discover, MasterCard, Visa
Remarks: Minimum stays during the summer season. No pets, fireworks, motorcycles, scooters, roller devices or off-road vehicles.

On the eastern slopes of Oregon's Cascade range, the ponderosa pine grow tall and stately, providing valuable habitat for deer, coyote, porcupine and raccoon. Eagles and osprey build their nests high in the pine's boughs, and squirrels, chipmunks and quail gather their seeds for food. At the 3,300-foot level, the pine give way to meadows and lakes, and it is here where Black Butte Ranch, Oregon's great golf and tennis resort, lies. The ranch is surrounded by seven Cascade peaks that range from the 6,415-foot cinder cone called Black Butte to the proud 10,495-foot Mount Jefferson. Sitting on the patios and decks of the ranch's condos and homes to watch the sun's first light on the meadow, you would be hard-pressed to tell where the ranch ends and the Cascades begin.

Not a Carbon Copy

Black Butte Ranch is a destination resort unlike any other. Each unit in the 1,830-acre development is individually furnished and privately owned, but many are managed by the ranch rental program. Carrie Larsen, who manages the rentals explains,"We offer deluxe hotel type rooms to one-two-and three-bedroom condominium units. For the vacationing family, we can also provide complete homes. Many of the units have fully stocked kitchens, washers and dryers, rock or brick fireplaces or wood-burning stoves, and all have televisions, telephones and wide inviting decks. Guests receive the same privileges accorded the owners - full access to two golf courses, four swimming pools,19 tennis courts, miles of bike and jogging paths, and the lodge." The lodge is a three-story glass, fir and pine building made a little more grand by the scale of the scenery outside its floor-to-ceiling windows. The furnishings combine antique tables

and secretaries with modern pine and fabric chairs. The rental accommodation desk and property sales office sets conveniently in the lobby area and the Lt. Henry Abbot and Elijah Sparks conference rooms, along with the restaurant comprise the main level.

On the uppermost floor, with an unrivaled view of the Cascades, is the lounge, where you can enjoy a full-service bar. Conference facilities and a highly qualified staff are available for small groups of up to 30 individuals at the lodge.

Ranchmade Specialties

The restaurant at the lodge, with its unsurpassed view of the mountains and overlooking Big Meadow, is renowned for its award winning cuisine. Ranch dinner specialties include generous cuts of prime rib, New York steak, roasted duck, fresh pacific salmon and fresh Oregon oysters. The wine list contains over 90 selections from Oregon, California and Washington.

Breakfast specialties include giant cinnamon rolls, eggs Benedict, and a farmers omelette. Lunch includes an assortment of deli sandwiches, salads, and a hot kettle of soup with fresh fruit. Banquet facilities for inside seating are available for up to 50 individuals and outside for up to 200.

The Sporting Life

Golf is the main recreational activity at Black Butte Ranch, which was awarded a silver medal by *Golf Magazine* as one of the top 50 golf resorts in the country. Residents and guests play on two 18-hole courses located amid the trees and within view of the mountains and lakes. Both Big Meadow, a 6,880-yard par 72, course and Glaze Meadow, a 6,600-yard par 72, course are open seven days a week in the spring, summer and fall. The facilities include a driving range, practice green and a pro shop at each course. The ranch offers golf clinics in the spring, along with golf packages. Golf professionals are available to assist you with your game throughout the summer.

If golf has a rival at the ranch, that rival's name is tennis. There are 19 Plexipave courts in seven different locations. The courts open at 7 a.m. for early risers. In addition to special instruction classes, guests can arrange for private or semiprivate lessons.

Swimmers have no problem cooling off on Oregon's hot, dry summer days, for the ranch has four large pools and several wading pools. Other activities include canoeing, horseback riding and whitewater rafting. There is great fishing on the Deschutes and Metolius rivers, or catch and release with barbless hooks on the lake near the lodge. The lodge has a good rental fleet of bicycles, since

The Main Lodge has the registration area, conference rooms and restaurant.

the ranch has carefully designed 18 miles of paved biking trails. In the winter, cross-country ski rentals are available at the Sport Shop.

We think so highly of Black Butte Ranch and all its well designed charms, that after many memorable visits, we intend to purchase a second home there and spend as much time as possible enjoying this very special place.

Sisters, the small Western town eight miles east of the ranch, has only three streets, yet more than 70 businesses, shops and restaurants line them. Known as the llama capital of North America, the community has become a center for llama ranches.

Getting There

From the north, drive to Redmond, then turn onto Highway 126 to Sisters. From the south, drive to Bend, take Highway 20 to Sisters. From the west, take Highway 22 from Salem, or Highway 126 from Eugene, which merges with Highway 20. The well-marked ranch turnoff is eight miles west of town.

THE HEATHMAN HOTEL

Address: S.W. Broadway at Salmon, Portland, OR 97205
Telephone: (503) 241-4100; toll free(800) 551-0011 for reservations
Location: Downtown in theater and shopping district
Host: Mary Arnstad, General Manager
Room Rates: $135 to $185 double; $175 to $375 one-and two-bedroom suites
Credit Cards: All major cards
Remarks: Weekend and specialty packages are available.

At a time when cities across the nation were bursting at their seams, yet ignoring the consequences of traffic and unplanned sprawl, Portland was tearing up freeways and planting parks. At a time when pollution was considered a fact of city life, Portland was turning to hydroelectric power and clean air, and restoring the Willamette River to ensure the purest drinking water in the country.

Rock of Revival

As modern spires began appearing on the skyline, the City of Roses encouraged the restoration of the l9th century architectural landmarks. One of the best of these was The Heathman Hotel. The new Heathman Hotel, as it was called when it opened in 1927, was showing the lines of age in 1984. Its solid 10-story brick exterior now reflects the city's more staid, provincial side of life. But once the doorman closes the glass entry behind you, the hand of noted San Francisco interior designer Andrew Delfino, of Stanford Court fame takes over, ushering you into a world of elegant residential comfort.

Oriental Flavor

The grand foyer has cool marble and polished teakwood. The hotel's subtle oriental flavor is evident throughout, including its Ming pieces and a rare rice paper Japanese Imari screen.

The resourceful concierge can assist you with transportation, secretaries, interpreters, a waterproof runner's guide, theater tickets, dining reservations and privileged access to nearby athletic clubs.

The hotel's 152 guest rooms and suites have all been designed with the needs of a discerning traveler in mind. From simple guest rooms to one and two-bedroom suites, the hotel can offer parlor suites with corner view living rooms for a variety of hospitality and business functions. There's a room for every need at The Heathman, all beautifully furnished and maintained.

Warm tones of terra cotta, celery and ivory accent the polished hardwood and contemporary rattan furnishings, which are covered in colorful English chintzes. King and queen-sized beds are available and rooms offer every conceivable amenity — private bars, television, 24-hour room service, plush bathrobes, Spanish soaps and bath accessories, and nightly turndown service.

Uncommon Services

The Heathman's mezzanine level includes a secluded library with signed first editions from renowned writers; a bar with bistro-style dining, which contains art pieces from the Elizabeth Leach Gallery, as well as a view to the Tea Court below. You'll find seven distinctive reception rooms for high level business meetings or private entertaining. The Symphony Room, with its fireplace, private service bar, is the perfect location for a pre-or post-event party to taste the excellence of Portland's performing arts. The Heathman's separate kitchen and private pantries can easily accommodate the needs of groups of 10 to 150 guests. The mezzanine has a private door, connecting to the Arlene Schnitzer Concert Hall, for hotel guests.

In the hotel's social Tea Court, two 17th century oils by Claude Gellee set the tone for the hand-polished gumwood panels, a multi-layered Austrian chandelier, a gracefully curving stairway, arched windows and a Steinway grand piano. This classic setting is our favorite place to meet friends for afternoon tea. The mood is one of relaxed sophistication, with lace-aproned hostesses serving finger sandwiches, scones and pastries along with The Heathman's special blended tea and other international teas, served with fine English bone china. Evenings of jazz are presented on Wednesday, Thursday and Friday in the Lobby Lounge.

Designer Dining

The Heathman restaurant has an enviable reputation for its local Oregon seafood, freshwater fish, game and other hand selected delicacies. Its snappy, energetic atmosphere is enhanced with Andy Warhol's "Endangered Species" animal art. For more casual fare, there's the Marble Bar, a great place from which to watch the activity on Portland's bustling streets.

Around the corner and up the block is the B. Moloch: Heathman Bakery & Pub. Its fun-loving decor highlights the work of 19th century French caricaturist, Henri Colomb. A 10-ton woodburning oven and specially designed smoke box add to the flavor of the cooking that has won the pub a loyal local following. After a day exploring, we often use the pub for take-out and bring our choices back to the quiet of our room.

The mezzanine level bar is decorated with original art.

In the Center of Things

The South Park Blocks area is home not only to The Heathman Hotel, but is the cultural heart of the city as well. The neighboring Performing Arts Center is host to the Portland Center Stage, an off-shoot of the award winning Ashland-based Oregon Shakespeare Festival. Two blocks away is the historic Pioneer Court Square, known as 'the living room' of Portland. Nordstrom, Saks and other fine retailers are close.

Getting There

From the north, Take Interstate 5 to the City Center Exit across the Broadway Bridge. Bear left on Broadway and go 16 blocks to the corner of Broadway and Salmon. The hotel is on the right. From the south, Take Interstate 5 north to Interstate 405 and continue on to the Salmon Street Exit. Go right on Salmon Street to the corner of Salmon and Broadway and make a right turn to the hotel.

GENOA

Address:	2832 S.E. Belmont Street, Portland, OR 97214
Telephone:	(503) 238-1464
Location:	Eastside of Portland
Hosts:	Kerry DeBuse, Joan Husman, David Burns and Catherine Whims
Cuisine:	Northern Italian
Prices:	Seven-course dinner, $45; four-course dinner, $36
Credit Cards:	American Express, Carte Blanche, Diners Club, Discover, MasterCard, Visa
Hours:	Seven-course dinner seatings from 6 p.m. to 9:30 p.m. on the hour and half-hour; four-course dinner seatings only at 5:30 p.m. and 6 p.m. Monday through Saturday.
Remarks:	Reservations recommended

Approaching the Genoa on your first visit, the last thing you expect to find inside is the warm light and rich color, wonderful aromas and gorgeous flowers that fill the restaurants dining area and accent the unpretentious, but elegant decor.

Genoa is known for its seven-course, fixed-price dinner. Part of the philosophy here is that the business of feeding people involves more than simply placing food, however carefully prepared, in front of them. Everything about the experience must be conductive to enjoyment of the meal.

The approximately two and one-half hour meal takes you on a leisurely tour of Northern Italian cuisine. The four senior cooks rotate duties semi-monthly; each is responsible for researching, designing, testing and preparing their feasts for a two-week period. The deliberate lack of hierarchy in the restaurant management creates an atmosphere of cooperation in which each person works with a sense of individual responsibility. Present owners Kerry DeBuse, Joan Husman, David Burns and Catherine Whims were employed by the restaurant, with a sum total of 50 years of Genoa experience, before purchasing it in mid 1992.

Northern Italian Experience

Year after year, Genoa has been highly esteemed by restaurant reviewers. Calling the food "truly great", the 1992 *Pacific Northwest Magazine* readers' poll named Genoa"The Best Restaurant in Oregon". But then, we have known that for years.

The meal begins with antipasto, which might be proscuitto and melon or in winter, bagna cauda, a hot fondue of cream, anchovy and garlic served with crisp vegetables and homemade sourdough breadsticks. An innovative soup, perhaps a savory cabbage soup or creamy soup of yellow summer squash, follows the antipasto.

Fresh homemade pasta comes next. The fish course may be red snapper with a mixture of mustard, garlic, anchovy and oregano, dipped in batter and sautéed in olive oil, or small filets of fresh tuna, marinated in extra-virgin olive oil, then charcoal grilled and topped with garlic mayonnaise.

Of seven courses, the only choices to be made are in the entrees and the desserts. Three entrees are always offered, including seafood, fowl and meat. Genoa's dazzling dessert tray features seven desserts, all of which are prepared fresh on the premises. A lengthy wine list offers Italian, French, California and Northwest wines.

Getting There

The Genoa is a 15-minute drive from downtown Portland. Go east over the Morrison Street Bridge (the street becomes Belmont). Continue about 25 blocks, Genoa is on the right side under a burgundy awning.

Here you can enjoy either a four or a seven-course Northern Italian dinner.

COLUMBIA GORGE HOTEL

Address: 4000 Westcliff Drive, Hood River, OR 97031
Telephone: (503)386-5566; toll free (800)345-1921; FAX (503) 386-3359
Location: On the western outskirts of Hood River, 61 miles east of Portland
Host: Lynne LaFountaine, Manager
Room Rates: $175 to $225 double
Credit Cards: American Express, Diners Club, Discover, MasterCard, Visa
Remarks: "World Famous Farm Breakfast" is complimentary for all hotel guests.

The mighty Columbia River surges at its feet. Majestic Mt. Hood soars at its back. Phelps Creek, which takes a final dramatic 203-foot leap to join the powerful river below, meanders through its 11 acres of flowered grounds. The Columbia Gorge Hotel has a most spectacular setting indeed.

This country inn is as rich with history as it is beauty. Oregon lumber magnate Simon Benson, prime mover behind the Columbia River Gorge Scenic Highway project and builder of Portland's Benson Hotel, saw the potential. In 1921, he opened the Columbia Gorge Hotel, a 42-room, three-story inn boasting "all with bath" and the state's only ballroom east of Portland.

Soon, the magic was felt and the hotel's reputation grew. In the midst of the Jazz Age, the Columbia Gorge Hotel became a favorite retreat for film stars and members of privileged society. Famous guests, such as Rudolph Valentino and Clara Bow, were said to have stayed here, some of whom even had rooms named after them. 1978 brought new owners, complete renovation, and the restoration of its historic title, "Waldorf of the West."

All That Jazz

The hotel's exterior, with red tile roof, warm yellow stucco walls and shuttered windows, is somewhat reminiscent of a Spanish villa. Inside, massive plastered beams, glittery chandeliers, swinging French doors and glass doorknobs give you a sense of the elegance of the '20s. Just off the lobby is the Valentino Lounge, a plush gathering place for sipping cocktails and enjoying music.

Each of the hotel's 42 rooms is different. Antique furniture and authentic replicas (gooseneck rockers, overstuffed chairs) create a warm, uncluttered look. Two rooms offer fireplaces, another features

an antique hand-carved wood canopy bed. Our favorites are rooms 239 and 339, which are directly above the Wah-Gwin-Gwin Falls.

The excellent hotel staff attend to your needs and see that there are no schedules, no unnecessary hurry and no rough edges to your stay; their belief is that your visit to the Columbia Gorge Hotel should be a time "out-of-time."

The hotel has become a respected host to corporate and private groups; the Benson Ballroom, with its removable dance floor, is ideal for meetings, banquets and weddings while the Falls Room is well suited for smaller groups.

Famous Food

The Columbia Gorge Hotel prides itself on its trademarked "World Famous Farm Breakfast," which was created during the Depression Era to provide a huge amount of healthy food for hotel guests. Today the care with which it is prepared and served makes it more than a nourishing meal—it's an event. Choose from more than 17 varieties of fruits that are displayed on individual dishes. Then enjoy a steaming baked apple, followed closely by a crock of oatmeal. Three eggs, ham, sausage links, bacon and hash browns are served with country biscuits and the famed "honey from the sky." Idaho trout is offered as an option to the pork meats. Save room for the stack of hotcakes because, as the menu says, you don't have to choose your breakfast—you get it all. Chilled champagne is also available.

The dining room overlooks the river. At night, in the soft candlelight, it becomes a romantic spot for enjoying a leisurely meal and watching the lights on the opposite shore. The excellent service is accentuated by tableside flambés and sautées. While the varied menu is largely game-oriented, featuring pheasant, rabbit, venison and lamb, it also includes delicious vegetarian and pasta dishes. Fresh Idaho trout and Columbia River salmon are also part of the Northwest regional cuisine that is prepared by Chef Brian Inaba in his innovative style. The wine list, with over 400 offerings, highlights wines from the Pacific Northwest in addition to a wide selection of California and French vintages.

Powerful Fun

The hotel is a wonderful base for the many activities found in this region. The gorge has become a mecca for windsurfers—westerly winds blow up to 60 miles per hour and an opposing current blows up to six knots, creating ideal conditions for skilled board sailors. From the hotel and other vantage points, you can watch the vibrantly colored sails jumping and jibing through the waves. Bonneville Locks and Dam, the first hydroelectric powerhouse in the area, offers

Two of the rooms offer fireplaces.

a visitor's center. Watch grain barges navigate the locks and, from April to October, see salmon climb fish ladders on their upstream journey. In the winter, the ski areas of Mt. Hood are easily reached from the hotel for a day of either cross-country or downhill skiing.

In spring, white apple blossoms blanket the slopes. By fall, rich harvests are en route to packing sheds. Try driving the Mount Hood loop, Oregon 35, and climb through orchards to supreme vantage points of the Columbia River below. Cross 4,157-foot Barlow Pass along one of the routes used by Oregon Trail pioneers in the 1840s. In spring, wild pink rhododendrons abound; in fall a profusion of vibrant autumn colors splash the hillside.

Getting There

Take Interstate 84 east from Portland and turn off at Exit 62. Cross the highway and turn left on Westcliff Drive. The hotel is ahead on your right. Amtrak offers service from Portland on the Pioneer and the hotel will arrange transportation from Hood River station.

SHELBURNE INN

Address:	4415 Pacific Way, Seaview, WA 98644
Telephone:	(206) 642-2442; FAX (206) 642-8904
Location:	One mile south of Long Beach on Long Beach Peninsula
Hosts:	David Campiche and Laurie Anderson, Innkeepers
Room Rates:	$85 to $155 double. Midweek off-season lodging packages available October through June.
Credit Cards:	American Express, MasterCard, Visa
Remarks:	Complimentary country breakfast with room. No pets. No smoking.

The Shelburne Inn, built in 1896, is the oldest continually operating lodging establishment in the state. Located on Washington's 28 mile Long Beach Peninsula, the inn was originally a mecca for Oregonians escaping the heat. Summer guests would steam along the river on a paddlewheeler to the Port of Ilwaco, then board a narrow gauge rail to Seaview. The existing structure is now on the National Register of Historic Places and has undergone a series of changes that includes the uniting of two buildings from opposing sides of the street in the spot where the inn now stands.

In the second of these two buildings, you'll find the nationally acclaimed Shoalwater Restaurant and the Heron & Beaver Pub, which serve lunch and dinner. In 1990, the Shelburne Inn was selected as one of the "10 Best Country Inns in America", in a nation-wide search sponsored by Uncle Ben's Rice. This is the only place we know in the rural Northwest where you can have this quality lodging experience combined with the world-class restaurant experience of the Shoalwater.

David Campiche, a Seaview native, and his wife, Laurie Anderson, decided to purchase the inn in 1977 and began renovation. Both are knowledgeable in antiques, and together they scoured England and Holland for the quality pieces that now fill the inn. In 1983, they completed a major expansion of the lower level and integrated Art Nouveau stained glass windows into the structure. A new wing added 5 guest rooms, bringing the total to 15. In February of 1992, Conde Nast, named the Shelburne Inn one of the 25 top inns worldwide, as chosen by the world's 25 most noted innkeepers.

Quiet Victorian Retreat

All of the rooms in the three-story inn have private baths; two rooms are suites. Hand-stitched quilts, crocheted pillow shams and

marble-topped dressers add distinction to each room, and antique brass bedsteads support firm, comfortable mattresses. Artwork gathered from Europe and from local artists blends gracefully on the walls, and most rooms open onto verandas bright with potted flowers. Upon arrival, fortify yourself for a tour of the area with the freshly baked cookies you'll find in your room.

The emphasis here is on ensuring that each guest's experience meets and exceeds expectation. If you want to visit, David and Laurie and their attentive staff are on hand to provide conversation, information on the area and ideas for recreation. If you want to relax and fade into the woodwork, there's room for that, too. Midweek and off-season, the Shelburne will gladly host retreats, meetings or reunions for small groups. The restful atmosphere is ideal for such gatherings and accommodates up to 30 people.

On a couple of large tables in the lobby, you'll be served a breakfast that *Washington Magazine* pronounced "the best in the state," but that we argue is one of the "best in the world." David, Laurie and their staff devote much of their energies to create a breakfast that sets a footnote for your entire visit. Prepared from a seasonal array of unusual indigenous foods, the choice of four entrées could range anywhere from oyster frittatas and homemade sausage to herb scrambled eggs kasari and pan-fried oysters. The whole family are mushroom collectors, and often strike out with Seaview resident and famous forager,Veronica Williams, in search of goosetongue and sea greens, and fresh wild watercress. The Shelburne's country-style feast has been featured in *Gourmet* and *Food and Wine*, and is complimentary with your room.

Year-Round Destination

Winter is a favorite time on the peninsula, when big storms hammer their way along the coast. Bundle up and beachcomb for Japanese fishing floats, driftwood and shells. The 28 miles of state-owned beach are perfect for favorite oceanside pastimes like kite flying and photography, and expansive wildlife refuges are located at both the north and south ends of the peninsula.

The Shelburne Inn is situated at the juncture of the Columbia River and the Pacific Ocean. From June through mid-October, this area offers some of the world's best salmon fishing. Surf and sturgeon fishing are also popular and productive here. Long Island's Willapa Bay is the cleanest estuary in the United States, and supplies the country with 25 percent of its oysters annually. Ask David and Laurie to show you where to find the biggest razor clams on the beach. Loomis and other nearby lakes are full of bass and trout.

If you have a canoe or kayak, you'll want to bring it along to explore Long Island in Willapa Bay. Tours are also available. You can hike

The Shelburne Inn is rated as one of the 25 top inns in the world.

for hours among the island's 247-acre stand of red cedars, which provide sanctuary for elk, deer, bear and the great blue heron. This is one of the last remaining reproducing climax forests that sprouted during a dramatic West Coast climate change 4,000 years ago. Thousands of years have passed since this island was hewn by the ocean from the Willapa Hills. Standing somewhere in the 8 miles of heavily forested wilderness, it seems like only a day has passed since that time.

Back on the mainland, horseback riding, tennis and golf are all within easy reach of the inn. Curio shops, museums and art galleries are great for browsing or picking up special gifts.

Getting There

From Seattle, take Interstate 5 south to Olympia, then Highway 8 and 12 to Montesano. Follow Highway 101 south to Seaview. From the Oregon coast, follow U.S.101 across the Astoria bridge and turn left to Ilwaco. Head north for two miles until you reach Seaview.

SHOALWATER RESTAURANT

Address:	4415 Pacific Way, P.O. Box A, Seaview, WA 98644
Telephone:	(206) 642-4142
Location:	In Shelburne Inn on Long Beach Peninsula.
Hosts:	Tony and Ann Kischner
Cuisine:	Northwest
Prices:	$12 to $22
Credit Cards:	American Express, Diners Club, MasterCard, Visa
Hours:	Lunch served in pub 11:30 a.m. to 3 p.m.; dinner 5:30 p.m. to 9:30 p.m. in both restaurant and pub; Sunday brunch (June 15 through September) 10 a.m. to 3 p.m. Open daily, except Christmas Day and December 1 through the 15th.
Remarks:	Reservations recommended.

The Shoalwater Restaurant shares what owner Tony Kischner describes as a "symbiotic relationship" with The Shelburne Inn. Linked by a couple of doorways, a strong friendship and a common spirit, the two businesses work in harmony to provide a complete dining and lodging experience.

Tony, formerly the manager of Seattle's legendary Other Place, and his wife, Ann, opened The Shoalwater in 1981. One hundred year-old stained-glass windows salvaged from a 17th century church in England have become the building's trademark. Tony blends the best of his international upbringing with his restaurant training to create a superb dining experience. Northwest foods are featured in a seasonally varied menu that changes every six to eight weeks.

Native Provisions

The Long Beach Peninsula is surrounded by three bodies of water filled with fresh fish and seafood. Willapa Bay is famous for its oysters and steamer clams; the Pacific Ocean yields bottomfish, crab and razor clams, while sturgeon and salmon stream through the Columbia River.

Chef Cheri Walker has been with The Shoalwater for all of its 11 years and combines these ingredients to create uncommon appetizers and entrees. "Cheri's a masterful chef who can produce flavor and match foods in unusual ways that come off marvelously," shares Ann. Whether you choose spring run Chinook salmon with cranberry and blueberry mustard sauce or poached oysters with saffron ginger in a beurre blanc sauce, you can still steal a bite of your companion's stuffed pork tenderloin in a shallot and garlic cream sauce. Starred menu items are low-calorie or low-cholesterol. Ann's homemade bread accompanies the meal, and her dessert tray merits the rave reviews and awards she has received.

"My one folly," is how Tony refers to the collection of over 500 wines the restaurant's features, a selection that has received the Wine Spectator's Award of Excellence. To showcase this diverse selection, Tony, Ann and Cheri hold one-of-a-kind dinners, part of their monthly Northwest Winemakers' Dinner Series. Held in the off-season, the meals emphasize regional foods that enhance the characteristics of wines from a particular winery; the winemaker is also in attendance.

The English stained-glass windows and dark, rich paneling of the Heron & Beaver Pub contribute to its atmosphere. A full range of single-malt Scotches and fine Cognacs leads the bar's complete selection, and Northwest microbrews are offered on tap. Lunch and light dinners are served in the pub throughout the year.

Getting There

From Seattle, take Interstate 5 south to Olympia, then Highway 8 and 12 to Montesano. Follow Highway 101 south to Seaview. From the Oregon coast, follow U.S.101 across the Astoria bridge and turn left to Ilwaco. Head north for two miles until you reach Seaview.

The award winning restaurant is within the Shelburne Inn.

EDGEWATER INN

Address: Pier 67, 2411 Alaskan Way, Seattle, WA 98121
Telephone: (206) 728-7000, toll free (800) 624-0670; FAX (206) 441-4119
Location: On the waterfront in downtown Seattle, at Pier 67
Host: Brian Rickert, Managing Director
Room Rates: $115 to $175 double
Credit Cards: American Express, Carte Blanche, Diners Club, Discover, Enroute, JCB, MasterCard, Visa
Remarks: Children under 18 free in parent's room. Non-smoking rooms available.

The most striking feature of the Edgewater Inn is the unobstructed view of Puget Sound through the floor to ceiling windows in the hotel lobby. Overhead a large chandelier, constructed from deer antlers brightens the room. The Edgewater is built entirely over the water on Pier 67, and is Seattle's only waterfront hotel. At one time a relatively nondescript hotel, the inn has been renovated with a warm Northwestern lodge feel, and the personal service and attention to detail that you'd expect of an elegant four-star establishment.

Managing Director Brian Rickert describes a visit to the Edgewater as "a real Seattle experience—if you were closer to the water, you'd be wet. Our guests can jog along the waterfront in the morning, come back and read the paper over a cup of coffee by the stone fireplace", says Brian. "It's a casual lifestyle that's easy to get used to." The lobby is filled with overstuffed chairs, friendly guests and is a great setting for coffee, cocktails or dessert served fireside. It's easy to imagine spending the day here, watching the sea lions and gulls play in Elliott Bay.

Rooms Around the Inn

The four-story hotel offers 238 guest rooms with outstanding views of Puget Sound and the Seattle skyline. Each has a private bath, television, overstuffed chairs, a table and a mini-bar. Many of the rooms that overlook the water have private balconies with chairs for reading or watching the ferries and tugboats crawl along. Large comforters in country plaid cover the double, queen- and king-sized beds, which are built by a local furniture company from white knotty pine logs. The warm country tones of the rooms are welcoming after a long day of meetings, sightseeing or exploring.

Business meetings and special events are handled capably and quietly for the comfort of all hotel guests. The inn offers seven meeting rooms and can accommodate up to 200 guests. Catering may be

arranged for conferences, weddings and other gatherings. Secretarial service and a full range of audio visual equipment are also available.

The hotel provides an exercise room, complete with a Lifecycle, Stairmaster, rowing machine and sit-up bench. For a more extensive work-out, the Seattle Club offers its complete fitness center to guests of the Edgewater for a daily fee. These facilities include an indoor lap pool, racquetball and squash courts, aerobics, a full range of fitness equipment and an indoor running track, massage, whirlpools, saunas and a tanning solarium.

Soundside Dining

Ernie's Grill is the main dining room at the Edgewater and features two walls of windows looking out over Elliott Bay that guarantee you a water view from anywhere in the restaurant. To ensure that you leave room for one of pastry chef Angela Schaeffer's desserts, you must walk past an elaborate display of her work on the way to your seat. Ernie's serves dinner nightly from 5 p.m. to 10 p.m. and features Northwest cuisine from homemade recipes, prepared simply but elegantly. Chef Leslie Dillon applies her northwest culinary training to create fresh regional specialties. Try Ernie's clam chowder to start off the meal, or share some Dungeness crab cakes. A variety of daily specials may include pan-seared Alaskan sea scallops, fresh San Juan Island king salmon or roasted honey, soy glazed duck.

In the morning, visit Ernie's Grill for a breakfast that ranges from pan fried French toast, eggs and waffles to the "Express Breakfast Bar," that offers assorted Continental breakfast fare. Lunch at the grill features a variety of soups, salads, sandwiches and special entrées. Next door to the restaurant is Ernie's Bar, which provides lunch, sandwiches and snacks throughout the day. Locals gather with hotel guests to watch sporting events on the big-screen television or to enjoy live music from a pianist or jazz ensemble, or perhaps a "jam session" with local musicians.

Extraordinary Fishing

Because of the Edgewater's location over the water, guests have been known to fish out of guest room windows. This practice was encouraged until people began to fish "seriously," and was discontinued altogether when an unsuspecting housekeeper found a mudshark swimming in a bathtub. Today, "fishing from the Edgewater" carries an entirely different connotation. A Seattle-based float plane lands in the sound, "the inn's back door," and carries you off to British Columbia for a day of unparalleled fishing. Charter flights are also available for golfing trips to any course that is accessible by float plane. If you prefer a leisurely cruise, the front desk staff can make arrangements for you.

The lobby overlooks the boat traffic on Elliott Bay.

The Edgewater's location is perfect for seeing Seattle's attractions. Just down the street are the Seattle Aquarium and the waterfront strip, filled with Native American art, seafaring curios and varied restaurants. Pike Place Market is 10 minutes away on foot, and the art galleries and shops of Pioneer Square are a five-minute trolley ride from the inn. A complimentary shuttle service is available to these and other locations. For joggers the inn is well located for long flat runs along the waterfront in both directions or good workouts climbing Seattle's hills.

Getting There

From the south on Interstate 5, take the Madison Street Exit and head west until Alaskan Way (about. one mile). Turn right onto Alaskan Way and drive one mile. The Edgewater will be on your left. From the north on Interstate 5, take the Columbia/James Street Exit and head west on Columbia Street to Alaskan Way (about one mile). Follow the signs to the waterfront.Turn right onto Alaskan Way and drive one mile until you see the Edgewater on your left.

INN AT THE MARKET

Address: 86 Pine Street, Seattle, WA 98101
Telephone: (206) 443-3600; toll free (800) 446-4484 (outside of Seattle)
Location: Downtown Seattle, in Pike Place Market
Host: Joyce Woodard, General Manager
Room Rates: $100 to $165 double; suites from $190; $15 per additional guest
Credit Cards: American Express, Carte Blanche, Discover, JCB, MasterCard, Visa
Remarks: Children under 16 stay free in parents' room. Non-smoking and handicapped rooms available.

Mardi and I celebrated our first anniversary here — in a room overlooking the majesty of the Olympic Mountains beyond Puget Sound and the eclectic energy of Pike Place Market below. The comfortable elegance of the Inn at the Market makes it an ideal spot from which to enjoy the environment of the market and downtown Seattle. Guests enter from the street into a quiet brick-paved courtyard, decorated with large flower pots. The courtyard muffles the sounds of the city and prepares you for relaxing and enjoying the inn's comfortable atmosphere and extremely personal service.

A visit to the inn offers a special experience. Its location in the middle of the vital, original public market is a much-coveted spot. The inn combines European country decor with a host of amenities: complimentary downtown shuttle service, refrigerators, honor bars, coffee makers with fresh ground coffee delivered daily, and evening turn-down service with complimentary chocolates. A basket of luxury bath amenities is waiting in the spacious, tiled bathrooms.

Of the 65 guest rooms, 45 offer a view of Puget Sound, the Olympic Mountains, a garden courtyard or the market. All rooms feature floor to ceiling sliding glass windows. Three parlor suites and the four townhouse suites offer the best vantage points on Seattle surroundings. Several one-bedroom suites are available for conversion into two-bedroom townhouses, where the parlor and one bedroom are on one level; the second bedroom is upstairs. An ideal layout for traveling families.

A fifth-floor rooftop garden deck offers a 180-degree view of Mount Rainier, Elliott Bay and the Pike Place Market below. Relax with a favorite person or a book in one of the comfortable Adirondack chairs that dot the deck, or watch the ferries make their way from island to island and back across the sound.

The inn's conference facility, the Victor Steinbruck Room, accommodates up to 20 people for boardroom-style meetings and comfortably entertains up to 50 guests for receptions. The inn will also provide catering for your event.

In the Inn

Select shops and services surround the courtyard. The Comfort Zone Relaxation Spa offers massage therapy, whirlpool, float tank and suntanning, all of which may be billed to your room. Another true Seattle landmark sharing the inn's space is the Cafe Dilletante. The famed chocolaterie provides specialty soups and sandwiches, espresso and incredible truffles and chocolate desserts. Room service for dinner is provided by Campagne, a French restaurant across the courtyard.

A Little Village

Despite its downtown location, outside the door of the Inn at the Market you'll discover the atmosphere of a small village. Just beyond courtyard and fountain is Pike Place Market, an old-time farmers' market where fresh fish stalls, vegetable stands and delicatessens stand amidst a chorus of merchants calling out in a dozen languages. Our out of town friends often have fresh salmon, crabs and clams packed to go. In 1971, the market was saved from the wrecking ball and became the focus of the Pike Place Market Historic District, a 7-acre area that is the symbolic heart of Seattle.

Seattle on Foot and Afloat

The Inn at the Market is ideally situated for shopping or exploring downtown Seattle. Shops around the market, major downtown boutiques and department stores are all within six blocks, and business travelers will also find major office buildings within short walking distance. The symphony, repertory theater, cinemas, opera and ballet are all easily accessible, and hotel guests may arrange transportation via hotel shuttle to any downtown location. A corner newsstand sells tabloids in several languages and magazines on most any subject imaginable. Neighboring art galleries display a variety of local and imported talent, and the brand new Seattle Art Museum is just four blocks away from the Inn.

Descending the stairs from the market, known as the Pike Hill Climb, you will arrive on Seattle's waterfront. Seafood restaurants, marine supply stores, import stores, the Seattle Aquarium and Omni Dome Theater line the busy wharfs. A tramway runs parallel to the water, offering easy access to the entire length of the district. Harbor tours are available from a number of operators along these piers.

Wake up to the enticing aromas of freshly roasted coffee and cinnamon rolls.

Washington state is proud of its ferry system. Passengers and cars travel across Elliott Bay and Puget Sound to the "bedroom islands" of Bainbridge and Vashon, and to the mainland port of Bremerton. Take a ride from Pier 56 to Winslow, on Bainbridge Island, for a half-hour cruise. Winslow offers a selection of shops and restaurants, and makes a pleasant afternoon or evening jaunt. Most Seattleites agree, there are few better spots from which to view the sunset over the Olympic Mountains than from the sundeck of the ferry.

For a slightly longer trip, pack a picnic basket and take the ferry to Bremerton. The round-trip ride will take you through the narrow pass on the south end of Bainbridge Island.

Getting There

From Interstate 5, follow Stewart Street west through downtown Seattle to First Avenue. Turn left onto First, travel one block to Pine Street and turn right. The Inn at the Market is on the right side of Pine Street. Valet parking is available.

ALASKA ADVENTURER

Address:	959 Harrison Street, Suite 140, Seattle, WA 98109 (reservations and information)
Telephone:	(206) 284-7648; FAX (206) 284-7672
Location:	From June to September, cruising the waters of Southeast Alaska
Host:	Captain Bob Horchover
Cabin Rates:	$593 for three days and two nights; $1,043 for a 10-day cruise.
Credit Cards:	Personal checks preferred
Remarks:	Includes fishing equipment, food and beverages.

Very few people have the opportunity to see the richness of the waters and glacier-altered coastlands of Southeast Alaska. Most who do, cruise through at over 20 knots, cocooned in large, urban cruise ships. While on their high speed pass, they are just skimming the surface of the real experience, which awaits those with the inclination to slow down and discover the sights, tastes, aromas and texture of this incredibly interesting area.

The southeast is a long knarly finger of land hanging down from the main part of Alaska. Along that creased finger are just a few cities and towns, and even fewer cars and roads. In fact, you can cruise for days and see very little, which is different than when the first explorers sailed these waters hundreds of years ago. Ashore you will find vast tree covered mountains, punctuated by staggering waterfalls. These lands still come with the original equipment of animals, most still un-spooked by the sight of man. The waters are clear, crisp and teeming with life. Humpback whales sound alongside, so close you can hear, as well as see, their breath. Porpoises ride the bow waves just beyond your touch, while eagles circle overhead watching the Orcas at play.

Explore In Comfort

The best way to discover the real southeast experience is cruise these waters with Captain Bob Horchover aboard his well-equipped 55-foot "Alaska Adventurer." If anyone knows how to elicit the things that are special about the southeast, it is Bob. He worked in the commercial fishing industry during college. While practicing dentistry in Juneau for 25 years, he continued to cruise and explore these rich waters. At one time he even had a dental office aboard, so he could offer his services to those living in the remote villages. Bob's skill and precision chairside have now been applied full time to sharing the area he knows and loves so much.

Everything is Provided

Bob built the M/V Alaska Adventurer with the sole purpose of taking small groups on custom cruises. Starting with a hull specifically designed for the Alaska waters, Bob created five comfortable state-rooms(some sleep three) and a spacious salon with large windows for easy viewing. He carries a professional chef and a seasoned crew. The boat is equipped with two 15-foot Boston Whalers for fishing and exploring. They take an average of eight and rarely more than 10 guests. The rate charged includes all the professionally pre-pared meals, the wine, beer and soft beverages, fuel, saltwater fishing tackle, bait and guides. You can choose to join a special focus trip or form a group of your own, of at least six, and have exclusive use of the boat.

The trips start in Juneau, but the real preparation starts months ear-lier when Bob begins to work with each group to make certain they receive the type of experience they are hoping for. For some, it is the chance to catch the large salmon and Halibut, for others the chance to be next to whales, and for others it is doing some hiking, seeing the animals and just relaxing.

A Close-in Experience

Your days are filled with cruising, sightseeing, fishing and explor-ing; the late afternoon will find you anchored in some small isolated cove. The crab pots are placed, cocktails are served with ancient crystal clear glacier ice and the evening's hors d 'oeuvres are pre-sented. It was just such a tranquil early evening when our friend, Bert, hooked a 168 pound halibut just off the stern of the boat. Imagine catching a fish who weighs as much as you do.

The dinners are generally three to four courses and may include heaping bowls of just-out-of-the-water Dungeness crabs, freshly caught fish, salads and desserts. In the summer it is light until after 11 p.m., so there is plenty of time for conversations, planning the next day's outings or viewing the videos taken hours earlier of the bear sitting on the near-by shore, watching you having breakfast.

The inclination for most people is to not plan enough time. We strongly recommend that you plan at least a week aboard. The area is vast, the sights incredible and the experience unforgettable. Then again, there is the magic. As Bob says, "Time and time again I have seen family groups or business associates come aboard tired, stressed and barely civil. After a few days they have relaxed, are doing new things and starting to enjoy each other again. By the end of the week, the magic has worked it's spell. Everyone has new ener-gy and appreciation for each other and more clarity for their own life goals . What they don't often realize is that they have just spent more

Days are filled with with cruising, sightseeing, fishing and exploring.

positive time together then they might have spent in the past several years. I've never seen the magic fail."

When you are done with your cruise, you will have been close enough to the whales to look them straight in the eye, have caught salmon larger then your nephew and have watched bears teach their children to fish. The southeast is now a personal experience, and like us, I bet it draws you back again.

Bob's season starts with a cruise north in early June and ends with the cruise back to Seattle in September. These 10-day trips cover the fabled "Inside Passage," with plenty of time for fishing and exploring. The rest of the year the Alaska Adventurer is in Seattle and available for party and short weekend cruises.

Getting There

Juneau is served by Alaska Airlines, Delta and Mark Air.

CAFE JUANITA

Address:	9702 N.E. 120th Place, Kirkland, WA 98034
Telephone:	(206) 823-1505; FAX (206) 823-8500
Location:	Eastside of Lake Washington
Host:	Peter Dow, Owner
Cuisine:	Northern Italian
Prices:	Entrees $13.50 to $21.
Credit Cards:	MasterCard, Visa
Hours:	6 p.m. to 10 p.m. daily
Remarks:	Reservations suggested.

Peter Dow describes himself as a "closet Italian." He is, in fact, owner of one of the Pacific Northwest's finest Italian restaurants, Cafe Juanita. Peter is also chief wine-maker for the house label, "Cavatappi," which is produced in his full-scale on-premises winery and served in the restaurant.

Natural Setting

Cafe Juanita is situated on Juanita Creek in the small community of Juanita, in Kirkland, near the northeastern tip of Lake Washington. The restaurant is surrounded by willow, maple and blue spruce trees. The natural setting is carried out inside as well, with muted lighting and warm beige tones set against a hardwood floor.

Buon Appetito

Unobtrusive chalkboards note the ever-changing list of entrees. Before you've reached the third item, someone is at your table to recite the menu in detail, taking time to colorfully describe each dish. Begin with an appetizer such as local steamed mussels or ravioli stuffed with gorgonzola and ricotta in a gorgonzola walnut sauce, putenesca (sun dried tomatoes, olives, capers and garlic over a delicate penne pasta) or smoked salmon on a spaghettini that is made fresh at the cafe daily.

Cafe Juanita offers eight to ten entrees nightly. A fresh fish selection, such as fresh halibut or swordfish grilled with olives, lemon and garlic, is generally available. Other entrees include "pollo a pistacchi" (chicken breast baked with proscuitto and parmesan in a pistacchio cream sauce) or "maiale saltimbocca", a pork version of the famous veal dish. Other meat selections may be "agnello arrosto" (lamb loin-chop marinated in garlic, olive oil and rosemary), or "spiedini misti "(skewers of assorted broiled sausages, chicken breast and garlic).

Entrees are followed by a dessert cart featuring homemade specialities, port and liqueurs. Cafe Juanita's own machine churns out fresh fruit gelati. Beneath the wisteria in the backyard, there is a small patio that holds five tables. On summer weekend evenings, Peter may host a special barbecue menu, but he won't know until that day if the weather will be suitable.

Peter's "Cavatappi" production has reached 700 cases per year. Known primarily for his Sauvignon Blanc, Peter also bottles a small amount of Cabernet Sauvignon. In 1987, he introduced the first Italian Nebbiolo grown in Washington, which is now in its third vintage. Cafe Juanita also stocks more than 250 Italian wines, and for the last several years Wine Spectator has named this prodigious cellar "One of the greatest wine lists in America."

Getting There

From Interstate 405 northbound, take Exit 20A and go west on N.E. 116th Street. After one mile, you will reach the main intersection of Juanita (116th and 98th Avenue N.E.). Continue through the intersection one more block to 97th and turn right at Spud Fish & Chips. The restaurant is one block straight ahead on the left.

Cafe Juanita has," One of the great wines lists in America."

THE HERBFARM

Address:	32804 Issaquah-Fall City Road, Fall City, WA 98024
Telephone:	(206) 784-2222
Location:	Half-hour east of Seattle in the foothills of the Cascade Mountains
Hosts:	The Zimmerman family
Cuisine:	Focus is on use of Herbs
Prices:	Six-course luncheon program, $42 per person; Nine-course dinners with five wines from $89. Classes available, priced free to $28.
Credit Cards:	MasterCard, Visa
Hours:	9 a.m. to 6 p.m. daily
Remarks:	Reservations required for restaurant. Free class schedule and catalog on request.

No visit to the Pacific Northwest is complete without an afternoon spent at The Herbfarm. Seventeen display gardens invite your wandering while the aromatic country store beckons with its large selection of books, dried wreaths, herbal soaps, herb seeds and teas. A good place to begin your visit to the Herbfarm is with a hosted tour of the walk-through gardens. The "Herbal Identification Garden" shows you herbs as they'll be when they mature at your home. .At the "Shakespeare Garden," the Zimmermans have planted herbs mentioned in Shakespeare's plays. Each is marked with the appropriate quote from the bard. The "Good Cooks Garden" entices you to try fresh herbs in your cooking. An "Oregon Trail Garden" grows all the herbs considered essential by pioneering women in the West.

Luncheons Fresh From the Garden

If you have a reservation for lunch, you proceed into the charming dining room. Tables are set with crocheted placemats and moss-green cabbage leaf underplates. Behind the tiled counter in the kitchen, Ron Zimmerman, chef Jerry Traunfeld, and staff are ready to start you on a three-hour culinary adventure. As the six-course meal unfolds, Ron, Carrie and crew interject bits of herbal lore, share culinary expertise, and generously divulge their recipes. Carrie weaves through the tables with herbs, giving diners a chance to pinch, smell and taste various herbs in their purest forms.

Menus are ever-changing as vegetables mature in the farm's gardens and as local fish and game come into season. Your meal might begin with herbal souffles in brown hen's eggs, to be followed by spring asparagus with wild morels and caraway greens.

An intermezzo of palate-clearing rose geranium and sweet cicely sorbet might lead to salmon with lemon verbena and tuberous begonia sauce, followed by The Herbfarm's "Salad From the Meadow's Edge" bursting with over 30 herbs, seasonal greens and edible flowers. The day's feast could conclude with lovage ice cream with purple sage sauce, coffee and your choice of over 17 herbal teas. A maximum of 30 people are hosted Fridays, Saturdays and Sundays from late April through the end of January.

A visit to The Herbfarm doesn't have to end when you leave, you can take plants with you and start your own garden at home. Herbs grown here are shipped all over the world, and are available for mail order through the farm's twice-annual catalogs. Be sure to sign the mailing list. The Herbfarm also presents over 300 classes each year on herbs for gardening, crafts and cooking.

Getting There

Take Interstate 90 east from Seattle to Exit 22 (Preston-Fall City). Go through Preston toward Fall City. At the "y" in the road after three miles, go over the green bridge onto 328th SE. Follow signs one-half mile farther.

Herb plants, shopping, gardens, 300 classes and fine dining await you at the Herbfarm.

BIRCHFIELD MANOR

Address:	2018 Birchfield Road, Yakima, WA 98901
Telephone:	(509) 452-1960
Location:	In Washington State wine growing region
Hosts:	Wil and Sandy Masset
Room Rates:	$60 to $90
Cuisine:	Classic international, regional and original specialties
Prices:	From $19 to $27 per person. Includes a four-course dinner, with homemade bread and chocolate. Wine, coffee and dessert are extra.
Credit Cards:	American Express, MasterCard, Visa
Hours:	Restaurant seating is at 7 p.m. on Thursday and Friday, 6 p.m. and 9 p.m. on Saturday. The manor is available for banquets and private parties of 12 or more Sunday through Wednesday.
Remarks:	Reservations required.

Birchfield Manor rests on six acres of land and was built in 1910 by a Yakima sheep rancher. In 1979, Wil and Sandy Masset purchased this 2-1/2 story Victorian home. After some initial remodeling, Birchfield Manor opened and began serving its memorable meals. After 10 years of popularity, the Massets decided to finish the remodeling and have added guest rooms to the upper floor of the manor. This makes the Birchfield Manor oe of the very few full country inns in Washington.

A World Class Restaurant

Chef Masset apprenticed at the Olympic Hotel (now the Four Seasons Olympic) in Seattle. He completed his training in Saint Moritz, Switzerland. Chef Wil combines regional specialties with classic, international flair, and the result is a wonderful blend of contemporary foods like loin of pork stuffed with eastern Washington goat cheese, served with hazelnut sauce— prepared in classic style.

Menus at Birchfield change weekly and each new menu offers a choice of five entrées, including fresh fish, steak, lamb,a chicken or pork dish and a special chef's selection. Each four-course dinner includes vegetables, manor-baked bread and chocolate. A recent menu offered an appetizer of chicken ravioli Florentine, maifun salad with almonds, Cajun-style sautéed pork tenderloin medallions with Cajun mushrooms and vegetable sauce, racks of Eastern Washington lamb, filet mignon, or breast of chicken with a red wine and raspberry vinegar sauce.

For a sweet ending, Chef Masset imports Callebaut chocolate from Belgium and makes the delicious truffles served at the end of every meal. He also sculpts chocolate, creating seasonal designs like sleighs and spring baskets. Fresh herbs grow in the manor's flower beds and their own hot house supplies the kitchen with lettuce, tomatoes, pumpkins and other vegetables.

Accommodating More Than Your Palate

Two years ago, the Massets extended their hospitality beyond the dining room and created five guest rooms on the manor's second floor. Each has a private bathroom, the English country elegance of antique furniture and new beds. After a day in the near-by wineries and a wonderful evening in the dining room, the ability to stay in the manor rounds out the experience. A swimming pool and spa behind the house are also available to guests.

Getting There

From Yakima, take Interstate 82 south to Exit 34. Take Exit 34 to State Highway 24, eastbound. Travel two miles. Turn right on Birchfield Road. The manor is the first house on the right.

This country inn is in the middle of the Washington wine growing region.

BRUSSEAU'S IN EDMONDS

Address:	Fifth and Dayton, Edmonds, WA 98020
Telephone:	(206) 774-4166
Location:	Old Town
Host:	Jerilyn Brusseau
Cuisine:	Northwest Regional
Prices:	Breakfast $1 to $3.95, lunch $2.90 to $5.75
Credit Cards:	MasterCard Visa
Hours:	Monday through Friday 7 a.m. to 6 p.m., Saturday 8 a.m. to 6 p.m., Sunday 8 a.m. to 4 p.m. in winter; one hour later in summer; open for breakfast and lunch only

brusseau's is located in Edmonds, the fashionable town brushing Seattle's northern fringe. It is a daytime place where the early morning air is scented with irresistible aromas from brusseau's own bakery. Local business people know to gather here for morning coffee and the sumptuous selection of baked goods from oatmeal raisin bread to raspberry cream cheese swirls. The cafe is also a lunchtime spot where people meet under bright Cinzano umbrellas for a sidewalk picnic, or around cozy tables inside for a warm, leisurely meal. On weekends, brusseau's is a great brunch spot.

Fresh and Local

Jerilyn Brusseau, owner and inspiration, is acclaimed as one of the Northwest's finest restaurateurs. We believe that is was Jerilyn's drive to find and serve the freshest local ingredients, which gave rise to the popularity of "Northwest Cuisine." As the menu says, "Everything at brusseau's is created to nourish not only the body but the mind and the spirit as well."

Bakery and More

brusseau's bakery produces nightly a wonderful selection of cinnamon rolls, pastries,breads and rolls. Lemon blueberry rolls and apple carrot banana bran muffins share the bakery case with a selection of cream cheese swirls, buttery croissants and huge cookies. Homemade pies, carrot cake and German chocolate brownies are among the daily dessert selections.

Breakfast specialties include Marionberry cobbler, creamy scrambled eggs with a muffin and fresh fruit, and ham and cheese croissants.Homemade quiches are found on the breakfast and lunch menus. Weekend breakfast is often accompanied by music performed by a local artist.

Lunch entrees and soups change daily, and are listed on a hanging chalkboard. Homemade soups such as "Duchess Vegetarian" warm a wintery day, while fresh salads are favorites any season.

Jerilyn and her cheerful staff handle brusseau's catering, including weddings, business meetings, picnics and other functions. We know they do an exceptional job, they catered our wedding reception with a wheel of creamy brie surrounded by a homemade crusty, cracked wheat braid and a huge carrot cake.

We never leave town, heading north, without a stop at brusseau's to create a picnic from among their bountiful selections.

Getting There

Head north on 1-5 and take the Edmonds-Kingston ferry Exit. Continue west into downtown Edmonds on Fifth Avenue. brusseau's is on the corner of Fifth and Dayton, across from the Old Mill Town. There is street parking available.

Everything is baked fresh daily.

HOME BY THE SEA

Address:	2388 East Sunlight Beach Road, Clinton, WA 98236
Telephone:	(206) 221-2964
Location:	On the southwest coast of Whidbey Island.
Hosts:	Sharon Fritts-Drew, Helen Fritts, Linda Drew Walsh
Room Rates:	$85 to $155 double
Credit Cards:	Discover, MasterCard, Visa. Personal and travelers checks preferred.
Remarks:	Room rates include full gourmet breakfast. Cottages provided with "Island Breakfast Baskets" and use of complete kitchen.

While traveling through Yugoslavia in the early 70s with her two young daughters, Home By the Sea's innkeeper Sharon Fritts-Drew emerged exhausted from a difficult bus ride. A kind woman gave them refuge in her home, where hot showers, good food and warm beds more than made up for the language barrier. This memory inspired the creation of Home By the Sea a year later, on the beach where Sharon had returned each summer for 20 years.

Home by the Sea is a place where Sharon encourages others to "take a pause from the hurried world." Your choice of lodgings includes the main house and six cottages, which are located within a five-mile radius.

At Home

The guest room faces west for a view across the bay to the Olympic Mountains.This sandy realm is home to eagles, geese, ducks and sandpipers. The Sunset Room has a queen-sized bed and private bath. Sharon has distributed her collection of American and European antiques throughout the guest room, interspersing work by local artists. The living room, with its broad picture windows facing the bay, has a multicultural flair, with an unusual Turkish copper tea set and carpets from Afghanistan.

In the morning, the home's cook brings in the most flavorful ingredients for breakfast. A farmer delivers eggs to the house for delicious eggs benedict, crepes and omelettes made with the garden's fresh herbs. Berries and apples are brought in from the garden to top rich Dutch babies. Poached pears from the inn's fruit trees and croissants from the island bakery round out this morning feast, which is delivered to your room. Just off the home is the Sandpiper Suite, with a private entrance, a queen bed and a kitchenette. Big country wicker

furniture fill the Sandpiper's beach-side sitting room, and the private deck offers spectacular views. In the closets hang plush bathrobes and beach towels for your trip to the private beachside jacuzzi.

▨ Not Inn

Home by the Sea's six cottages offer atmosphere and seclusion. Each has a fully equipped kitchen stocked with a special "breakfast basket" filled with farm fresh eggs, fruit, granola, breads and muffins, Home by the Sea's private label jam, cheese, milk, tea, coffee and juice. Tables are pre-set with elegant china. Wood and kindling are provided for each place.

Just down the road from the Home by the Sea is the 1940s Cape Cod Cottage. A perfect family retreat, with two double beds, a child's single and a crib. The cottage is furnished with American antiques circa 1940. We love the Japanese deep soaking tub.

The Nordic Cottage, three miles away, overlooks quiet Lone Lake. The lake is known for excellent trout fishing in summer and ice-skating in winter. The Nordic's wood-burning stove, Danish lace curtains and hardwood floors create a romantic getaway.

Sequestered in a deep forest five miles away is the Swiss Chalet, decorated with floral print wallpaper and French lace curtains. To add to the warmth of the wood-burning stove below, eiderdown comforter covers the queen bed upstairs. Skylights admit starlight and a new jacuzzi completes the experience.

The Cameii Cottage is a one-bedroom cabin on a private beach. The bedroom, full kitchen and small living room comprise the comfortable interior of this campy abode, and a fold-out futon in the living room provides extra sleeping accommodations.

The French Road Farm is on 10 acres of land, divided between meadow and deep forest. Furnished in French and American country antiques, the farmhouse has a large bedroom with a queen-sized bed; a reading room and a comfortable couch that folds out into a queen-sized bed. From your vantage point in the 7-foot jacuzzi, you can watch deer and small animals come into the meadow to graze.

Across the road from the farmhouse is Island Greens Golf Course, styled after a course in Scotland. This par-three, 9 hole course is open to the public, and if you plunk your fee into a milk can that's chained to a nearby tree, you can play all day.

Whidbey Island is the longest island in the contiguous United States. On the southwest corner of the island, tucked under Double Bluff, is Useless Bay. At low tide, the beach stretches bare for a mile, endearing itself to beachcombing.

The main house is on the beach at Useless Bay.

Nearby Merkerk Rhododendron Gardens is a special treat for flower lovers. From spring through summer, grand bushes reaching 20 feet in height display brilliant flowers of all shades. Coupeville, located mid-island on Penn Cove, is one of the oldest towns in the state. It features Victorian homes, an 1855 blockhouse, and specialty shops and restaurants. Tours are available.

Getting There

Drive north on Interstate 5 from Seattle to the Mukilteo—Clinton ferry, Exit 189. Drive four miles to the ferry landing and board the Washington State ferry for a 15-minute ride. Head north on Highway 525 for six miles to Bayview center. Turn left on Howard Road and left again on Bayview Road. Continue one mile to Sunlight Beach Road and turn right. Continue to the end of the road; the inn is on the left.

THE INN AT LANGLEY

Address:	P.O. Box 835, 400 First Street, Langley, WA 98260
Telephone:	(206) 221-3033; FAX (206) 221-3033
Location:	Whidbey Island, on Saratoga Passage
Hosts:	Sandy and Stephen Nogal, Innkeepers; Pam and Paul Schell, Proprietors
Room Rates:	Guest room $155; corner guest room $175; suite $225
Credit Cards:	American Express, MasterCard, Visa
Remarks:	Rates include complimentary Continental breakfast buffet. All rooms and restaurant are smoke-free. Children 12 and over are welcome. No pets.

Selected as one of "The Top 10 Country Inn's of America," in the nationwide contest sponsored by Uncle Ben's Rice, The Inn at Langley wins our vote for having the nation's sexiest bathrooms. When you come out to see the rest of the inn, you'll find it's not only an ideal location for a romantic weekend, but also for corporate gatherings or for a quiet weekend alone.

The inn's 24 rooms are separate enough to ensure privacy, but they lend a sense of being part of a greater entity. A world of wildlife shares the environment, whales swim the passage, eagles soar in the sky and heron stalk through the marshes. All contribute to the gentle peace you'll find on the island.

The inn combines elements of the natural Northwest with the under-statement of Asian design. The colors of the beach and the feel of the forest have been brought inside, creating harmony between the interior and the outdoors. Peeled pine poles accent sand-colored walls. Nubby, neutral carpeting simulates Japanese woven mats. Private decks with upholstered benches overlook the water and are dotted with colorful flowers and shrubs.

The innkeepers, Sandy and Stephen Nogal, are ever-present and attentive to the needs of their guests. With several years of experi-ence in the hospitality business, the couple is well-equipped to han-dle the details of operating the inn. "We want to share this quietly rich place with you," says Sandy. The Nogal's careful attention is evident in the list of amenities they provide. Each room has a fire-place, and televisions, refrigerators and coffee brewers are standard features. The spacious bathrooms have large showers and over-sized jacuzzis. The bathrooms have windows facing out to the sea, or back into the room and the warm light of the fire. Plush towels and thick terry robes are provided for your stay.

All rooms have spectacular views that span at least 180 degrees, and the six corner rooms offer an even more expansive range of vision. Two suites provide separate sleeping arrangements and a sofa-bed in the living room; two of the four floors are wheelchair accessible.

The inn has a conference room that accommodates up to 20 people boardroom style. Eighteen-foot ceilings and a view of the passage contribute to the relaxed atmosphere. Audiovisual equipment is also available, including an electronic projection screen.

The inn's environs are a blend of Northwest woods and edible gardens. Lanky vine maples stretch skyward in lightwells. Fruit trees and berry bushes flank the grounds. On the street level, a Japanese-style waterfall flows quietly over two tiers of rock.

Country Kitchen

The large country kitchen adjoins the dining room. From this open kitchen, innkeeper and chef, Stephen, produces an abundance of good food. A drop-in buffet breakfast is offered to all guests. Steve's freshly baked muffins accompany the inn's favorite muesli, fruit and locally made preserves.

Diners congregate around the long Frank Lloyd Wright-designed cherry table for lively conversation, or one of the smaller tables lining the room. A river-rock fireplace dominates this dining room.

Steve serves dinner Friday and Saturday nights. This five-course, prix fixé meal features Northwest ingredients such as salt marsh lamb, forest morels, winter blackmouth salmon and fresh loganberries. "We try to use local ingredients that reflect the island's offerings," says Steve. He is happy to share his recipes, and we always come home with several favorites to add to our collection.

The inn's wine cellar is built into the foundation of the kitchen. Focusing on wines from the Northwest, the 3,500-bottle cellar also includes selections from California, Europe and Australia. Wines can be ordered to accompany dinner or to enjoy in the guest rooms.

Island Exploration

Primarily rural, Whidbey Island deserves investigation, and Langley is a great place to start. Langley is a casual seaside village with a historic rusticity. Unique shops feature local art and handiwork, and you can find antiques, gifts and books in various small, sophisticated stores. A half-dozen restaurants are within walking distance of the inn featuring casual bistros and Mediterranean cuisine. For a bit of local flavor, drop into the Doghouse Tavern for a beer. Grocery and liquor stores are also close by. Guests who enjoy outdoor activities can choose to bike, fish or ride horses.

Each room has a water front balcony

At Greenbank, Ste. Michelle Winery maintains the Whidbey's Liqueur distillery. In the tasting room, you may sample this unique beverage made from local loganberries.

Stephen and Sandy have discovered the best places for watching sunsets, no matter what the season. They will gladly share their secrets and suggest some romantic sites for private picnics along the beach or in the island forests.

Getting There

From Seattle, take Interstate 5 north to Exit 189 (Whidbey Island-Mukilteo Ferry), following signs to ferry landing. Boats depart every half-hour. Arriving Clinton, follow State Highway 525 north to Maxwelton Road. Turn right. Proceed to the end of the road. Bear left onto Langley Road. Continue on to Cascade, which becomes First Street. The inn is on the right.

TURTLEBACK FARM INN

Address: Route I, P.O. Box 650, Eastsound, WA 98245
Telephone: (206) 376-4914
Location: Six miles from Orcas Island ferry landing in Crow Valley
Hosts: Bill and Susan Fletcher, Innkeepers
Room Rates: $70 to $150
Credit Cards: MasterCard, Visa
Remarks: No smoking inside, no pets, no infants. Children by special arrangement.

Turtleback Mountain swells up from the west lobe of Orcas Island, one of nearly 172 islands in Washington state's San Juan archipelago. Orcas' interior is comprised of valleys, ponds and meadows. It is overlooking one of these meadows, that you'll find Turtleback Farm Inn. The setting is serene, complete with grasslands a barn and outbuildings, 300-year-old maples and six ponds, one stocked with trout (catch and release).

Completely renovated by Susan and Bill Fletcher in 1985, the restored 100-year-old farmhouse has the charm of a country manor, accented with warm woods and a fresh uncluttered decor. Hanging on the wall inside the front door is an ad from the September 22, 1933, Seattle Daily Times featuring the film Tarzan the Fearless. The ad reads, "Buster Crabbe, muscular Olympic swimming champion, whose latest screen appearance brings excitement aplenty to the Roxy Theater." The famous actor is Susan's father.

A Touch of Class

Each of Turtleback's seven individually decorated guest rooms reflect the Fletchers' careful attention to detail. All are special, from the Meadow Room with its expansive view, to the Nook, which is reminiscent of a ship's cabin. Spotless Northwest fir floors throughout the inn are softened by imported rugs. Floral print cottons envelope wooly comforters—the wool is directly from the backs of the sheep you see grazing outside. The living room is a cozy gathering place for inn guests.

Fresh Start

Dining room tables are set with fresh white linens, fine china and silver, and a turtle-shaped trivet with a pot of freshly ground coffee or brewed tea. On pleasant mornings, breakfast is served on the sundeck, which is surrounded by a ring of trees and overlooks a

meadow full of geese. Fresh juice and fruits begin the meal. During the summer, there are fresh berries from the island, and the fall brings apples from the trees right on the farm. Next comes Susan's famed granola. As diners crunch along, Susan is busy preparing the next course, which may be ricotta pancakes with fresh berry sauce, eggs Benedict or smoked salmon buckwheat crèpe gateau. Celtic harp music wafts in from the kitchen as guests begin their Orcas day in fine fashion.

An Orcas For Everyone

Guests may walk from the farm Inn into the meadows below. Domestic chickens, ducks and geese share the land with several varieties of migratory birds. The forests, pastures and meadows are home to the farm's flock of sheep and grazing Charlois cattle.

A visitor to Orcas will not leave Turtleback Inn without a map of the island, complete with Fletchers' heiroglyphics denoting points of interest, as well as some personal advice on what to see and do. Fishing is always a favorite sport as Orcas' waters are an obliging host to salmon and cod. As Bill says, "These are some of the richest waters I've seen." Bicycling, sailing, canoeing and kayaking are common island activities. A walk along the beach at Obstruction Pass is a prime way to view soaring eagles or perhaps the dorsal fin of an Orca whale disappearing into the sound, —there are 3 resident Orca pods who live in these rich waters year around.

Cascade Lake at Moran State Park is a wonderful place to stretch out after a long sleep at Turtleback. In addition to swimming, the lake offers trout fishing from small rental boats, or a chance to try out the paddle boats.

Hikers will enjoy the two mile walk around Cascade Lake. There are over 23 miles of hiking trails in Moran State Park. An easy quarter-mile walk through the forest brings hikers to Rustic and Cascade falls. For the more ambitious, Mt. Constitution awaits—its 2,409 feet create a challenging hike to the highest point in the San Juan archipelago, but the view is well worth the effort. For those with ease in mind, you can drive to the top and limit your hiking to the stairs of the monument at the summit.

Midweek and off-season visitors will experience the true flavor of the island. Crowds are down, the pace is slower, and there is more of the island's charm just for you. Fall colors brighten the landscape.Winter comes with its own mood, complete with storms and misty nights and spring brings the pastels of flowering plants and trees.

Returning to the inn's welcoming fire is a fine way to end the day. On the corner game table, in the living room, an intricately carved chess

Susan's wonderful breakfasts get guests off to enjoy Orcas Island.

set with mermaid queens and ship's mates for pawns invites a challenging match. Guests are invited to use the wet bar, which is always stocked with special teas, coffees and cocoa.

Bill and Susan live in a separate home on the farm, so in the evening when they retire to their home, guests can experience having the entire farmhouse to themselves. This is an ideal situation if you come with your own group during the off-season and occupy the entire inn. The seclusion of the inn has proven to be an ideal atmosphere for small meetings and planning sessions.

Getting There

Orcas Island may be reached by a float plane service from downtown Seattle. You may take the Washington state ferry from Anacortes with your car or as a walk-on passenger. Upon arrival on Orcas, drive 2.5 miles on Horseshoe Highway. Turn left at the road sign that indicates Turtleback Farm Inn. Travel one mile and turn right on Crow Valley. Continue nearly 2.5 miles, the inn will be down on your right.

CHRISTINA'S

Address:	Main Street, Eastsound, WA 98245
Telephone:	(206) 376-4904
Location:	On Main Street in Eastsound, Orcas Island
Host:	Christina Gentry Orchid
Cuisine:	Natural Northwest
Prices:	$12.50 to $17.50
Credit Cards:	American Express, Carte Blanche, Diner's Club, MasterCard, Visa
Hours:	6 p.m. to midnight daily June 12 to August 15. 5 p.m. to 10 p.m. Thursday through Monday the rest of the year. Brunch served Sunday from 9:30 a.m. Closed New Year's Day to Valentine's Day.

This little hamlet on the shore of Orcas Island's Eastsound Bay seems an unlikely spot for one of the state's top-rated restaurants. Eastsound's Main Street runs little more than four blocks and houses only a single structure taller than one story. That building is the Island Union Building, and its second story contains Christina's, a cozy restaurant with a broad view of the the bay.

Orcas Island is but one in the chain of San Juan islands. One of the largest islands, it sports a year-round population of nearly 1,500. Eastsound is the hub of culture and cuisine. Both visitors and locals alike recognize Christina's as "the" restaurant on the island.

Natural Northwest Cuisine

Christina selects and prepares the meals herself. Fresh, locally grown products include seafood from the cold waters of Puget Sound, oysters from the island, mussels from nearby Lopez Island, poultry and lamb from Lopez.

All meals are prepared with simplicity and distinction. Few sauces, if any, are used in most dishes, reflecting Christina's strong belief that the natural flavors of the food should remain pure. "This is what I call natural Northwest cooking," she says. "I want to serve only fresh local products as simply and purely as is possible." For instance, the restaurant's generous serving of poached salmon is glazed with basil then served with a fresh garden salad, fresh vegetables and just-picked new potatoes.

The menus change with the season and the readiness of the natural ingredients. The poultry may be pheasant, game hen or chicken. The meat may be a different cut each evening. A specialty is the rich

Christina's bouillabaisse, lavishly packed with fresh, local shellfish and served with one of the 50 or 60 regional wines.

Christina's desserts bring meaning to after-dinner treats. She serves fresh berry tarts or, homemade ice cream, such as lavender honey and espresso and homemade pina colada cheesecake.

A former art student, Christina takes pride in her collection of Oriental rugs, copperware and old kitchen implements almost as much as she does her culinary skills. The restaurant is a blend of both talents. Each table has a direct view of the bay; the blue table-cloths capture and extend the colors of the sea. Fresh flowers and chic china add elegance to the setting. Oil lamps provide soft light, blending with the setting sun. There is a marvelous postage-stamp-size lounge off of the dining room for dining, or relaxing over a drink before or after the meal.

Getting There

In Eastsound, the two-story Island Union Building is easily recogniz-able; turn into the adjacent alley and walk up the stairs.

Christina selects and prepares all the meals herself.

Western
Canada

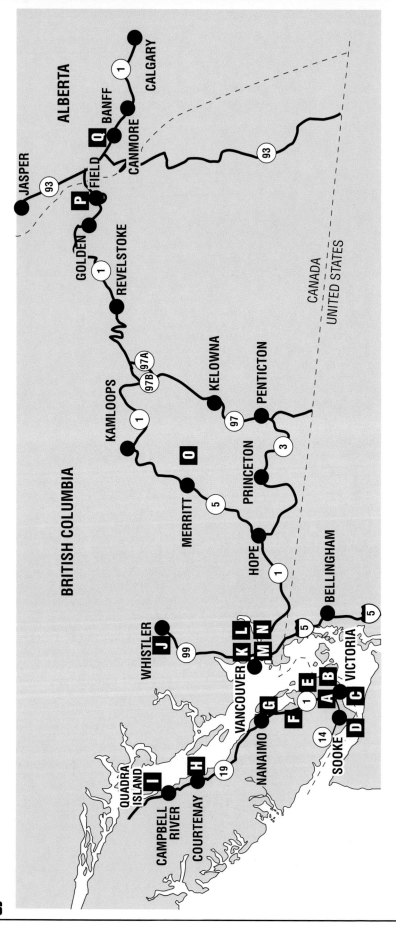

ALBERTA

CALGARY

1

BANFF

Q

CANMORE

93

FIELD

P

93

JASPER

GOLDEN

1

REVELSTOKE

97A

97B

KAMLOOPS

KELOWNA

PENTICTON

1

97

BRITISH COLUMBIA

O

3

MERRITT

PRINCETON

5

HOPE

1

BELLINGHAM

CANADA
UNITED STATES

5

WHISTLER

J

99

K L

M N

5

VANCOUVER

1 E

A B

VICTORIA

5

F

C

NANAIMO

G

D

14

SOOKE

19

H

COURTENAY

QUADRA
ISLAND

I

CAMPBELL
RIVER

WESTERN CANADA SPECIAL PLACES

A   Holland House Inn

B   Abigail's Hotel

C   Chez Daniel

D   Sooke Harbour House

E   Oceanwood Country Inn

F   The Aerie

G   Yellow Point Lodge

H   Old House Restaurant

I   April Point Lodge

J   Durlacher Hof

K   Park Royal Hotel

L   Corsi Trattoria

M   Teahouse Restaurant

N   Seasons in the Park

O   Hatheume Lake Lodge

P   Emerald Lake Lodge

Q   Buffalo Mountain Lodge

HOLLAND HOUSE INN

Address:	595 Michigan Street, Victoria, British Columbia V8V 1S7
Telephone:	(604) 384-6644; FAX (604) 384-6644
Location:	Downtown Victoria, two blocks from the Inner Harbour
Hosts:	Robin Birsner and Lance Olsen, Innkeepers
Room Rates:	$115 to $185 (Canadian), $25 per additional guest; includes full breakfast.
Credit Cards:	American Express, Diners Club, MasterCard, Visa
Remarks:	No pets. Smoking restricted to balconies. Children not encouraged. Handicapped accessible.

If fine art and a little bit of the avant-garde is in your blood, the Holland House Inn in Victoria is sure to tickle your fancy. Stepping into the Holland House is like stepping into a contemporary art gallery. Imagine clean painted walls, a black granite fireplace, French doors to the patio, and expansive windows that flood the room with sunlight. Then picture abstract watercolors, vibrant oils, charcoals, line drawings and unusual free-form sculptures— not traditional works of art, but bold, modern, bizarre, even political pieces bearing the signatures of host Lance Olsen and other noted artists in the area. Welcome to Victoria's exclusive "fine arts hotel."

Lance Olsen, a native Englishman, and his wife, Robin Birsner, a former Southern Californian, are the minds, talent and energy behind the artful bed-and-breakfast inn. We were impressed with the fact that they, personally, cook, clean and attend to their guests with all the hospitality one could imagine. In 1986, using their carpentry and decorating skills, they gutted and transformed an old apartment building into the visually stimulating Holland House Inn. One of Lance and Robin's main goals in creating the inn was to create a place to display their endless private collection of contemporary art.

An accomplished artist, Lance has shown his work at the Victoria Art Gallery and international art exhibitions all over the world. Now he essentially has his own gallery, where he can still create and work in a field he also enjoys, Lance does a show every two to three years.

A Touch of Class

The inn is a two-story building located in James Bay, Victoria's oldest residential area. Encircled by a stylish white picket fence and surrounded by flowering trees, manicured lawn and colorful flower beds, the Holland House is a eclectic collection of furnishings

inside. Hardwood antiques, and upholstered armchairs mix surprisingly well with art deco fixtures and modern pieces in wicker and cane. An elegant guest lounge on the main floor, complete with herringbone oak floor, serves as a gallery, gathering place and breakfast area all in one. The art pieces, of course, are what make the Holland House so delightfully unusual. We found Lance's work and the sculptures by David Toresdahl especially entertaining.

The Holland House features 10 guest rooms, each one a masterpiece of its own. All of the rooms are spacious and offer queen-sized beds, private baths with deep soaking tubs, fluffy goose down comforters and color televisions. Each is distinct in its decor and appropriately decorated to complement the paintings, sculptures or hand-painted pottery pieces that dominate the room. All but one of the rooms have French doors leading out to private balconies or verandas. Cozy sitting areas offer a quiet place to enjoy your breakfast if you prefer the privacy of your room. Our room, like a few others, came with a romantic fireplace and four-poster bed. Fresh-cut flowers from the garden added that special touch.

In the off-season, the Holland House Inn can accommodate groups or business meetings of up to 25 people. The lounge makes a wonderful meeting spot or groups may reserve the entire inn.

Breakfast is Served

From 7 a.m. to 9 a.m., guests are treated to a beautifully prepared breakfast. You may join others in the lounge or, with a soft knock on your door, welcome the Holland House's exquisite room service. Be prepared to begin a day in Victoria with one of five entrees, including sunny baked eggs with ham, brie and fresh parsley, or German apple pancakes in a puffed pastry topped with yogurt and maple syrup. Lance and Robin are also known for their muesli made with fresh apples and bananas with grated nuts, as well as their tasty oatmeal spiced with nutmeg. Homemade granola, and muffins and scones hot from the oven are also sure bets.

In the Middle of Town

The inn is conveniently located between downtown and the spectacular harbour, with its view of the Olympic Mountains. Some sights to see include the nearby Parliament buildings and tourist center, the famed Empress Hotel and the British Columbia Provincial Museum, with its impressive collection of native art and artifacts as well as information about the area that spans 25,000 years. You can hop a tiny 10-passenger ferry that will take you around the harbour and drop you off downtown or at Fisherman's Wharf.

Breakfast can be taken in the privacy of your room.

If you've had enough walking for the day, a romantic horse-drawn carriage will gladly pick you up at the inn and carry you through town. Other activities include a visit to the colorful Butchart Gardens, cycling, guided fishing excursions, and kayaking in hand-built wooden crafts.

Lance says the best part of visiting Victoria is taking things slowly. Nearby Beacon Hill Park, which overlooks the water, offers 75 acres that are just perfect for that. If your visit has you in Victoria during April or May, ask about the Jazz Festival and the Swiftsure Race, which attracts boats and people from all over the world.

Getting There

From the Seattle Clipper terminal (in front of the Empress Hotel), proceed south on Government Street two blocks, past the Parliament buildings. Take a right onto Michigan Street. The inn is directly to your left, on the corner of Government and Michigan streets.

ABIGAIL'S HOTEL

Address: 906 McClure Street, Victoria, British Columbia
                 V8V 3E7
Telephone: (604) 388-5363; FAX (604) 361-1905
Location: A few blocks from the heart of Victoria
Host: Bill McKechnie, General Manager/Owner
Room Rates: $112 to $215 (Canadian); $26 per additional guest.
                 Mid-week rates from mid-October to mid-April
Credit Cards: MasterCard, Visa
Remarks: Rates include breakfast. No Pets. No Smoking.

The name Abigail means "a father's joy." Abigail's Hotel, the brain-child of owner Bill McKechnie is indeed a joy. Nestled in a quiet neighborhood, with a carefully manicured garden, this European-style inn has been extending its charms since opening in 1985. A copy of a Rodin sculpture of a young woman wearing a straw hat with flowers rests on a table inside the front door. "This sculpture," Bill says, "was the influence for Abigail's theme."

Unique Perspectives

Abigail's interior is a geometric masterpiece. Angled archways and vaulted ceilings create unique perspectives on the traditional Tudor design. Surprise nooks, notches and crannies add a humorous touch and evoke a childlike sense of discovery. Soft peach, rose, teal and ivory tones are used throughout the inn, tastefully woven into a peaceful quilt of color.

Abigail's Hotel is set on a quiet residential cul-de-sac. Its four stories offer a broad selection of secluded rooms, and we like the fact that there is no elevator serving the three floors. Most of the rooms feature fireplaces, and in two of these, the fireplace is glass enclosed and adjoins the bathroom and living area. In these rooms you can relax in a deep soaking tub while watching the fire. Abigail's ever-service-minded staff keeps rooms stocked with wood so that all guests can easily light a fire on chilly evenings.

Extraordinary service and attention to detail really are the bench-marks of this establishment. Upon check-in, an innkeeper will show you through the hotel, introducing you to its various rooms and amenities, addressing your questions about where to shop or what to visit along the way. The knowledgeable staff has long tenure with the inn and you can rely on their recommendations on the area.

The library is the primary gathering place for the inn's guests. Stately burgundy couches center around the fireplace. The walls are

lined with leather-bound volumes to keep you occupied until the sherry and hors d'oeuvres are served at the daily social hour. The library is also the ideal spot for small receptions and weddings.

Eight guest rooms offer private jacuzzis, complete with fluffy terry-toweled pillows for total relaxation. The spacious tiled bathrooms feature pedestal sinks and brass fixtures—establishing an elegance that is echoed in the crystal chandeliers, eyelet curtains and antiques in each room. Goosedown duvets accent comfortable beds, and several rooms have refrigerators. One of our favorite things about the hotel is the addition of little "breakfast doors" to some rooms. Your breakfast may be passed in from the hall, set on a shelf inside the wall, for you to pick up at your leisure, eliminating all rushing around and looking for robes. There are no televisions or telephones in the rooms, but a phone is located near the front desk.

Abigail's Breakfast

A cheery breakfast room shares the main floor with the library. Light oak tables, a brick fireplace and lace curtains create a welcoming atmosphere. Coffee is available starting at 7:30 a.m.; breakfast is served from 8 a.m. to 9:30 a.m. The big, open kitchen is an inviting spot to watch the cook preparing breakfast as you coax open groggy eyes with a steaming mug of coffee.

The inn's cook prepares a delightful meal from the open kitchen and leans over the counter to chat with guests. For starters, freshly baked muffins or coffeecake wait in baskets on the table. Enjoy these with some of the inn's delicious homemade jams, prepared on a farm on the Saanich Peninsula. Next, the cook prepares you one of Abigail's specials- eggs Florentine, baked eggs with smoked salmon and asparagus, or perhaps a seasonal omelette.

In the Heart of Victoria

Abigail's location is ideal for exploring Victoria on foot. Whether you arrive by jet catamaran, ferry or plane, you'll be within easy reach of almost anywhere you want to go. If you drive to Victoria, your car will have a pleasant "vacation" as well, as most sights and attractions are within easy walking distance. Just three blocks to the north, on Fort Street, there is a broad assortment of antiques shops, for which Victoria is known. Auctions take place Tuesday and Friday evenings, and are likely to produce a real find for the collector. It's also an easy walk from the hotel to the wharf area.

Stroll along Government Street near the Inner Harbour for a look at many of Victoria's shops. Munro's Books, one of Canada's largest independent bookstores, displays its many volumes in a restored

Each room is individually decorated and goosedown duvets cover the beds.

historic building. Straith's, also on Government Street, is noted for its fine tailored clothing. Irish linens, tartans and native British Columbian art are among the many other local wares.

A short drive form Abigail's, on Rockland Street, is the Lt. Governor's Mansion. The well-maintained grounds are open to the public. Visit the Art Gallery of Greater Victoria, which features one of the finest Japanese art collections in Canada. Nearby is the Craigdarroch Castle, built in 1851 by Robert Dunsmuir for his wife. The castle has 36 rooms and leaded glass windows imported from Italy. Don't miss the opportunity to visit the world famous Butchart Gardens.

Getting There

From the Inner Harbour, head north on Government Street. Take an immediate right onto Humboldt Street. Continue four blocks to Vancouver Street. Turn left onto Vancouver and continue 4 blocks to McClure. Turn left. Abigail's is at the end of the cul-de-sac.

CHEZ DANIEL

Address: 2522 Estevan Avenue, Victoria, British Columbia V8R 257
Telephone: (604)592-7424
Location: In residential northeast Victoria
Host: Daniel Rigollet, Owner Chef de Cuisine
Cuisine: Classic French with Nouvelle Cuisine
Prices: Entrees $11 to $19.50 (Canadian)
Credit Cards: MasterCard, Visa
Hours: 5:30 to 10 p.m. Tuesday through Saturday.
Remarks: Closed Sunday, Monday and Canadian holidays.

The inauspicious exterior of Chez Daniel may be somewhat misleading. Tucked in a small group of up-scale shops on a quiet street of northeast Victoria, the pained windows and lace curtains are only vague clues as to what awaits inside. Chez Daniel is an intimate, very sophisticated, very French restaurant owned and operated by Daniel Rigollet. He also prepares its cuisine. Chef Daniel is a member of the world's oldest guild for masters of cuisine, the Confrerie de la Chaine des Rotisseurs; his meals are the culmination of his culinary experience in France, Switzerland, Germany, Ireland,the Netherlands and Canada.

Daniel combs the Victoria markets early each morning to obtain his high quality ingredients. His prevailing attitude: continually strive toward perfection. The charming, gracious chef uses only the freshest foods, and the quality is evident in his dishes.

Two candlelit dining rooms, each decorated in a muted palette of mauve and teal, accommodate an intimate number of diners. Baroque music and rich kitchen aromas create a pleasing atmosphere. Guests are greeted warmly; the waitstaff upholds the finest standards of service, delivering a cheery "bon appetit" with the commencement of your meal.

Very Fresh, Very French

Begin with one of Chez Daniel's appetizers such as fresh sauteed mushrooms, escargots with garlic butter, sweetbreads with mushrooms and port in a puff pastry. Daniel's "soup a l'oignon, au gratin" is a fresh rendition of the traditional soup. Salad with hearts of palm and artichoke is the perfect intermezzo before the main course. "Salade Caesar" is artfully prepared at your table.

Daniel's broad selection of entrees may make it difficult to choose just one. Salmon with Noilly Prat and cream, and fresh trout with almonds lead the fish section. Fresh prawns sauteed in butter and topped with tomato and a dash of garlic is another popular selection. A special "Rable de Lapereau `Hussarde" (loin of rabbit) is prepared for parties of two, and young rabbit in a white wine sauce is a delectable alternative. Fresh lamb with a ginger, shallot, brandy cream sauce is one of Daniel's favorites.

Chez Daniel's wine list includes some 290 selections from Australia, California, Canada, France and Germany. Fine champagnes round out the cellar. Homemade fresh fruit sorbets are an excellent, light finale. A tray of cheese, mostly imported, is offered in keeping with the French tradition.The dessert tray is hard to resist, though, with its chocolate truffles, creme caramel Chantilly, and floating islands. Teas, including herbal blends, and espresso cap off the evening. Chez Daniel also serves a variety of dessert "special" coffees, including the "Chez Daniel" cafe, with five liqueurs.

Getting There

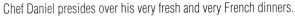

Take Fort Street east, it becomes Cadboro Bay Road. Continue to Estevan Avenue and turn right.

Chef Daniel presides over his very fresh and very French dinners.

SOOKE HARBOUR HOUSE

Address: 1528 Whiffen Spit Road, Rural Route 4,
Sooke, British Columbia V0S 1N0
Telephone: (604) 642-3421; FAX (604) 642-6988
Location: Twenty-three miles west of Victoria
Hosts: Fredrica and Sinclair Philip
Room Rates: Approximately $130 to $235 (U.S.)
Credit Cards: American Express, En Route, MasterCard, Visa
Remarks: Breakfast and lunch included in room rate.
Reservations recommended. Lunch served to hotel
guests only. Wheelchair accessible guest room.

If ever an inn was created to lull life's tempo back to a natural ada-
gio, it's Sooke Harbour House. This trim, white elegant inn rests just
above Sooke Harbour's Whiffen Spit, and through the inn's picture
windows you'll have a sweeping view of the Strait of Juan de Fuca
and Washington's Olympic Mountains. Look down, and an ever-
changing landscape of tidal pools, kelp beds and natural driftwood
sculptures create a living mural.

Stitching the many fabrics of Sooke Harbour House together are
Fredrica and Sinclair Philip. Fredrica, born in Cannes, France, radi-
ates a refined warmth. Dressed in her crisp French frocks, she gra-
ciously manages the workings of the inn as well as the raising of
their four children. Sinclair is a native of Vancouver and holds a
doctorate in political economics from the University of Grenoble,
where he and Fredrica met. He is well-studied in wines and foods,
and an expert Northwest seafood chef.

World Class Dining

Colorful gardens ring the inn; pansies, pineapple sage and
Corsican mint are among the inn's 400 varieties of herbs, flowers,
berries and fruit trees. I was initially surprised to see Sinclair snatch
a crimson petal from a rose and take a bite out of it, until he
explained that over 95 percent of the gardens on their grounds are
edible and most of it ends up on the menu. The ocean realm also
offers a prodigious array of delicacies, from octopus, sea urchin and
gooseneck barnacle to periwinkles and whelks. Under the spell of
Sooke's masterful chefs, the land and sea gardens blend to create
the freshest and most innovative cuisine in British Columbia. The
renowned national guidebook, Where to Eat in Canada, has just
awarded the inn's restaurant three stars as one of Canada's top 10
restaurants for the seventh consecutive year, and *Country Inn's
Magazine* named it one of North America's top 10 inns.

Daily Sea Harvest

Here, when they say "seasonally," they mean "daily." Fredrica is a strong advocate of providing food only in its proper season, so although you won't find strawberry on the menu after strawberry season ends, you won't have a chance to miss it. Sinclair is an avid scuba diver and takes full advantage of the rich bounties of their watery front yard for each evening's meal. The local fishing fleet supplies fish and crab to create a menu that changes every day. Sinclair, Fredrica, David Feys and other talented chefs share in the preparation and presentation of the meals.

Fresh sea urchin roe and fresh sea cucumber may appear as appetizers. Fresh steamed sablefish with an anise-hyssop butter sauce, or fresh skate sauteéd with a cranberry vinegar sauce may be among the choice of entrées. More traditional seafood dishes are always available, as are local, organically grown meats such as rabbit, veal, lamb, duck and suckling kid.

Ideal for Honeymoon and Romance

Sooke Harbour House, like its cuisine, is an exquisite mingling of traditional North American country sensibilities and West Coast native design. The New House, offers 10 distinctly different rooms. Each is named and decorated with a theme, and all have an expansive ocean view and private balcony or terrace. In each room, a comfortable sitting area faces a woodburning fireplace that is stocked and ready to light.

One of the most coveted rooms is the Victor Newman Longhouse, named for the Sooke carver of its many Indian masks and a rare hand-hewn Chieftain's bench. This large room features a king-sized bed and bathtub for two. The tub is situated next to a see-through fireplace that lends a view of Sooke Bay and the mountains beyond. The Mermaid Room and the Underwater Orchard both have decks with outdoor whirlpools and stunning views through their own private gardens by the ocean. The Icthyologist's study, sometimes referred to as the "Fish Room," is a veritable aquarium of fish art, including hand-painted fish tiles, fish prints, fish rubbings, and fish weavings. As in many of the other rooms, hand-painted tiles are also found in the Edible Blossom Room, where taking a shower can be a botany lesson in disguise.

The main house bears all the charm of an airy French auberge. The three upstairs bedrooms are furnished with antiques, handmade flower wreaths and handsewn quilts. They also offer fireplaces and whirlpool tubs for two. The split-level Blue Heron Room features a king-sized bed, spacious sun deck, and perhaps the best view from the inn while in the whirlpool tub for two.

The Victor Newman Longhouse Room has museum quality carvings.

With no disrupting television and the lull of ocean waves, Sooke provides absolute respite from the outside world. Good food, good beds and long walks in nature erase lines from your forehead and schedules from your mind. Begin with a walk along Whiffen Spit. Bald eagles nest nearby, while herons, sandpipers, loons and cormorants frequent the area. Killer whales, seals and sea lions feed just offshore as well as the "resident" grey whale. The inn's staff will arrange scuba diving, kayaking, or windsurfing equipment and fishing charter rentals. The West Coast Life Saving Trail and Pacific Rim National Park begin at the road's end near Port Renfrew and extend nearly 100 miles along the coast.

Getting There

From Victoria, take Highway 1 north to the Highway 14 intersection. Follow signs to Sooke. Approximately one mile from the stoplight in Sooke, turn left onto Whiffen Spit Road. Follow it to the water, where the Sooke Harbour House is on your right, at the ocean's edge.

THE AERIE

Address:	P.O. Box 108, Malahat, British Columbia V0R 2L0
Telephone:	(604) 743-4055; FAX (604) 743-4766
Location:	25 minutes north of Victoria on the Scenic Malahat Drive
Hosts:	Maria and Leo Schuster
Room Rates:	$130 to $290 (Canadian); includes full breakfast.
Credit Cards:	American Express, MasterCard, Visa
Remarks:	Main floor is wheelchair accessible. Children not encouraged. Restaurant open to public for dinner 6 p.m. to midnight Sunday through Friday, 5:30 p.m. to midnight on Saturday (closed Monday evenings during the off-season). Six-course dinner, $49 (Canadian); reservations advised.

Not unlike a falcon's aerie perched high within the cliffs, Maria and Leo Schuster's "Aerie" sits high above the Trans-Canada Highway and commands a bird's eye view of the awe-inspiring fjords and Gulf Islands below. We find it difficult to describe the vista from The Aerie's window-lined dining room. The spectacular sunsets melt into darkness pierced only by the moon, stars and twinkling lights of Victoria and Port Angeles in the distance.

The Aerie is just as impressive as its picture-perfect backdrop. Open since May 1991, the clean white stucco building, set off by its clay tile roof, bright green awnings, romantic balconies and windows, resembles a Mediterranean villa. The interior is elegant, featuring hand-carved furniture, original oil paintings, and a collection of rugs from around the world. The inn, however, is probably best known for its exquisite dining. Chef Leo Schuster brings with him 30 years of worldwide culinary expertise.

Heavenly Hosts

Owners and innkeepers Maria and Leo Schuster, both originally from Austria, recently came to Victoria from the tropical Bahamas. When they discovered this property high above the Malahat, Leo says there was instantly no question where they would retire. But what started as an idea for a simple bed-and-breakfast inn blossomed into a more than full-time labor of love that has pushed retirement further into the future.

Neither Maria or Leo are newcomers to the hotel trade. In the Bahamas, Maria owned and operated an exclusive resort. She grew up in the hotel business and was the first female manager of a luxury hotel. Leo's experience in the culinary world spans 30 years,

cooking in Europe, the Middle East, in Canada and on cruise liners. To come to Victoria, Leo left his job of seven years as the executive chef at Donald Trump's Resort International casino on Paradise Island in the Bahamas. His colorful past has had him preparing dishes for Queen Elizabeth, Richard Nixon, Henry Kissinger and former Egyptian President Anwar Sadat.

Grace and Grandeur

The Aerie is a blend of grace and grandeur. The 14 rooms reflect Maria's eye for decorating and details. Guests are greeted with a fresh fruit basket and fresh-cut flowers in their rooms. All of the rooms are individually decorated, many with hand-crafted Italian furniture, vaulted ceilings, private jacuzzis, fireplaces and balconies with that unbelievable view. All of the rooms offer queen- or king-sized beds and private bathrooms.

Guests also enjoy the use of a large hot tub, sauna, sun deck and library. The inn possesses conference facilities that will accommodate up to 14 people, ideal for executive gatherings. The hilltop is also home to a helicopter pad; bring your own or ask the Schusters to help you arrange helicopter transportation. Newly opened is a chapel for weddings and a large partially covered deck for receptions and outdoor dining.

Breakfast is served to only the overnight guests. In fact, the inn is open to the public only during the evening hours, assuring complete privacy during the day. Prepared with precision are morning omelets, poached eggs, fresh fruits and European style pastries and other dishes.

A Six-Course Extravaganza

The dining room is Leo's forte. Its white tablecloths, fine silver, china and crystal are crowned by an impressive 23-carat gold-leaf ceiling. A pianist, tucked away in the corner of the room, adds a classical flare. The atmosphere is elegant, romantic and intimate. And the 180-degree view from the dining room is one that would be difficult to find elsewhere.

Dinner at The Aerie is a six-course extravaganza. The menu changes every few days, as Leo buys only what is fresh and seasonal. His menu features recipes from 'round the world as well as 90 wines from a well stocked cellar. For starters, guests may choose from a couple of appetizers that could include smoked sockeye salmon with avocado and quail eggs, a hot terrine of scallops, or "zakuski," tart appetizers from Russia. Two or three soups on the menu will be followed by a salad course. The dinner entrees range from roasted rack of lamb with honey and rosemary to breast of duck with elephant garlic and ginger to seafood dishes such as fresh East Coast lobster or Dover sole.

The inn has incredible views down into the bay waters below.

Beef entrees may include filet mignon, pepper steak or medallions of veal with red onion marmalade. The night we dined at The Aerie, the dessert menu featured port marinated strawberries with chocolate creme, apple croustande with minted creme anglaise, and chilled cheese souffle with raspberry coulis. Last, but not least, guests are treated to Kona coffee or tea.

Other Sights, iF You Must

The Schusters have scattered tables and chairs along the nature trail that winds through the 5 acres. If one is compelled to leave The Aerie to explore, however, the inn is only minutes from the highway, which can lead to golf, sailing, swimming, fishing and boating.

Getting There

Travel north from Victoria (or south from Duncan) on the Trans-Canada Highway to the Spectacle Lake Provincial Park turnoff. Take the first park turnoff, then follow the sign straight ahead to The Aerie.

OCEANWOOD COUNTRY INN

Address: 630 Dinner Bay Road, Mayne Island, British Columbia V0N 2J0
Telephone: (604) 539-5074; FAX (604) 539-3002
Location: On Mayne Island, an easy ferry ride from Victoria or Vancouver
Hosts: Marilyn and Jonathan Chilvers
Room Rates: $95 to $150 Canadian (October through April); $99 to $170 (May through September).
Credit Cards: MasterCard, Visa
Remarks: Rates include breakfast and afternoon tea. Children 16 and over welcome. Two-night minimum stay on weekends, three nights on holiday weekends. Smoking permitted in library and on outside decks. No pets.

Geologically speaking, the Gulf Islands of Canada are a continuation of the American San Juans. Situated between Vancouver Island and the mainland of British Columbia, the chain includes five or six larger, inhabited islands and some just big enough for a beach chair. Somewhere in between is Mayne Island, a quiet rural community with a permanent population of less than 800 people. Whether you arrive by ferry, private craft or sea plane, the trip to Mayne Island is just long enough to give you a chance to shrug off real-world worries and to slide into the contentment of the countryside.

For years Marilyn and Jonathan Chilvers spent the holidays in their waterfront cottage on Mayne Island, taking a break from demanding advertising and public relations careers. Engaging in a common island activity—wandering around—in 1989 they came upon a large Tudor house for sale overlooking Navy Channel. Gradually, the idea of opening a bed and breakfast inn took hold of the Chilvers and soon the house was transformed into Oceanwood Country Inn. Complete with a full-service restaurant, the inn opened to the public in April of 1990.

Hearthside

If you've left your car behind, Jonathan will meet you at the ferry and drive you to the inn. On the way, he'll fill you in on island history, area attractions and activities. The house is at the end of a winding drive. After a warm greeting from Marilyn, you can settle down by the fire in your room or wander into the living room for some conversation with your hosts. Take a deep breath, as the Chilvers maintain, "stress is a word that is banished from our lexicon."

The house offers plenty of common space for sitting around and relaxing entirely or, if you have business to attend to, accommodates meetings of up to 12 in a fully equipped boardroom. The games room features over 25 games, ranging from the 3,500 year old "Nine Men's Morris," to more modern diversions. Marilyn and Jonathan maintain a diverse collection of books and magazines for your enjoyment, and the comfortable sofas in the library offer quiet places to read. Outside you can wander in the garden, which supplies fresh herbs and vegetables to the restaurant, and is carefully protected from local deer who would drop by for dinner without reservations.

Of the inn's eight guest rooms, seven have queen-sized beds; one offers two twins. Rooms are named and decorated after flora and fauna found on the island. Each room has a private bath and a wonderful water or garden view. The Rose Room is one of the most stunning rooms, with an open marble fireplace and a whirlpool bath from which to watch the snapping of the fire. From the room's private balcony you'll have a clear vantage point of the bay, where you may see eagles fishing. A terrace with a large hot tub overlooks Navy Channel. Three of the inn's guest rooms open onto this terrace. Two of them, the Kingfisher and Heron are also equipped with fireplaces and whirlpool baths.

Freshly Seasoned

Included with your night's stay is your morning repast in the inn's fine restaurant, usually served by Marilyn and Jonathan. In the intimate dining room you'll find a variety of cold cereals, yogurt, fruit, fresh coffee, tea and juices. Oceanwood's fresh baking yields delicious coffeecake, scones, croissants and muffins, and the hot entree changes daily. Among these you may find scrambled eggs with gravlax, buttermilk pancakes with apple compote and sausage or orange French toast with bacon. To stave off afternoon hunger, tea is served at four o'clock in the games room, with a variety of cakes and cookies to hold you over until dinner.

The restaurant at Oceanwood seats 30 fortunate diners, and is open to the public for dinner. This is an exceptional four-course, prix fixe meal that Jonathan says "changes endlessly and upon the whims of the chef." Chris Johnson is the culinary craftsman who brings his experience with Vancouver's Pan Pacific and Four Seasons hotels to bear, using local produce and other fresh seasonal ingredients to create one-of-a-kind dinners. Tomato Dungeness crab soup may start off your meal, followed by an appetizer of mushroom and goat cheese ravioli au gratin. Herb and garlic pork loin with rhubarb and lemon confit leaves just enough room for a chocolate almond cake with raspberry coulis. Choose from a wide array of Northwest wines to complement dinner, featuring fine labels from British Columbia, Washington, Oregon and California wineries.

The Rose Room is one of eight comfortable guest rooms.

Space to Collect Your Thoughts

Mayne Island is not well-known for its entertainment industry. Marilyn notes, "People come here to wind down, spending a little quiet time in the country. A big day might involve going for a bike ride along country lanes (the inn provides four bikes for its guests), walking on the beach before tea, then settling down for a nap." You might also want to allow time for a sauna in your busy schedule. It is a pleasant 45-minute walk from Oceanwood to the local market, and a pub is just down the street if you're up for some fish and chips or a pint of ale.

Getting There

Oceanwood Country Inn is served daily by B.C. Ferries from Tsawwassen and Swartz Bay, and by a scheduled float plane service from Vancouver or Victoria. Arrangements can be made to meet guests at the Mayne Island ferry terminal.

YELLOW POINT LODGE

Address: Rural Route 3, Ladysmith, British Columbia V0R 2E0
Telephone: (604) 245-7422
Location: On the water eight miles north of Ladysmith
Host: Richard Hill
Room Rates: $94 to $159 double (Canadian); $52 per additional guest. Mid-week reductions of 20 percent, October through April. American Plan.
Credit Cards: MasterCard, Visa
Remarks: No pets. Guests 16 and over welcome. Two-day minimum stay on weekends, three-day minimum on holidays. Rates include all meals.

On the eastern coast of Vancouver Island is a promontory known as Yellow Point. There, over 50 years ago, Gerry Hill built a lodge and created a refuge from the stress of city life. His first lodge burned down in 1985, and has since been rebuilt with a similarly impressive design and with the same loving attention as the original lodge. Coming by land, you'll travel a long, narrow dirt road that runs through a thick unspoiled forest. The lodge is at the road's end on the rocks overlooking the water.

At capacity, in the summer, Yellow Point Lodge never has more than 100 guests, which means you'll never feel crowded. You are free to enjoy all 180 acres and explore over one and a half miles of beach that make up the property. Simplicity and hospitality are the driving forces behind the popularity of this eccentric resort. Hill intended his home to be a sanctuary for friends and strangers, for the wildlife and the trees. Gerry's son, Richard, carries on this tradition, personally attending to his guests, the lodge and property.

Of the resort's accommodations, nine private rooms in the lodge and five new cabins offer the most modern conveniences. Several cottages offer separate bedrooms with private baths while others are geared for more adventurous experiences, with no running water and camp-style communal washrooms. Richard Hill says, "Yellow Point is comfortable but not fancy. It's not for everyone, but if you like meeting friendly people and feeling at home in a natural and beautiful place, you'll like it here."

In addition to muffins just out of the oven, breakfast includes hot and cold cereals, a buffet of fresh fruit and juices, followed by a full breakfast with eggs any style, bacon, sausages and pancakes. Lunch is served buffet-style, and may be turkey in puffed pastry or chilled salmon. Homemade soups and a variety of salads accompany homemade breads and rolls.

For dinner, a fisherman may pull up to the new dock at the lodge and unload fresh salmon. Barbecues are also frequent dinner events.

Off-Season Attractions

In the summer, the lodge fills up early, but mid-week and off-season accommodations are more easily arranged. Although the summer months provide weather conducive to a wide range of outdoor activities, we prefer the off-season. In the fall, dozens of different migratory birds arrive in the area, and as the winter rolls in, activity along the shore picks up, with sea lions, eagles and killer whales.

Getting There

From Vancouver, take the new ferry route from Tsawwassen to Nanaimo or the Horseshoe Bay ferry to Nanaimo, then drive south on Route 1 about five miles to Cedar Road. Follow the signs through Cedar to Yellow Point, about 10 miles. From Victoria, drive north on Route 1 and proceed toward Ladysmith.Three miles beyond Ladysmith, turn right on Cedar Road and follow the signs to Yellow Point Lodge.

The massive log lodge faces the water.

THE OLD HOUSE RESTAURANT

Address: 1760 Riverside Lane, Courtenay, British Columbia V9N 8C7
Telephone: (604) 338-5406
Location: On the bank of the Courtenay River
Host: Michael McLaughlin, Proprietor
Cuisine: Continental
Prices: Entrees $10.95 to $17.95 upstairs and $4.95 to $13.95 downstairs (Canadian)
Credit Cards: American Express, MasterCard, Visa
Hours: 11:30 a.m. to 9 p.m. daily, upstairs opens at 5:30 p.m. and closes Sunday and Monday (Monday in summer only). Sunday brunch10:30 a.m. to 2 p.m.
Remarks: Reservations upstairs strongly recommended.

The town of Courtenay, in the beautiful Comox Valley, is situated midway along Vancouver Island's eastern flank. Here along the Courtenay River in 1973, Michael McLaughlin purchased the pioneer Kirk Family home, on four acres, and transformed it into a premier dining spot, The Old House Restaurant.

"At the Old House," says Mike, "we aim to create an all-around enjoyable experience, which includes the grounds, buildings and people. Food is the primary reason people come here, but the surroundings certainly enhance the whole feeling."

The Old House is essentially two restaurants sharing one roof. Entering on the ground floor, one is reminded of a lively English pub. A stone fireplace and heavy beams lend a lodge atmosphere. Meals are moderately priced and feature robust pub-style sandwiches, burgers, salads, pastas and local seafood specialties.

Upstairs one finds a more elegant dining room, lit with coal-oil lanterns and warmed by a fire. Open timbers are accented by skylights and hanging plants. Leaded windows offer views of the river and the grounds.

Up or downstairs, you will receive some of the best Canada has to offer. All the produce is locally grown. Island farmers provide the poultry and livestock. The Old House also provides its own house-smoked meats. Its bakery produces fresh bread and desserts daily and the gardens bring forth a fresh supply of herbs and flowers.

During our last visit , we enjoyed the Japanese chicken consomme with dungenous crab dumplings, followed by salad of smoked rabbit on butter lettuce, with fresh local berries, asparagus and pinenuts. A main course of sauteed lamb medallions, seasoned with seven grains and finished with a sauce of fresh mint and chives. An extensive international wine list is available featuring European, Canadian and American vintages. The Old House offers lunch selections such as gourmet salads, soups, sandwiches and intriguing items like seafood pepper stirfry, with sauteed shrimp, calamari, baby clams, scallops, bell peppers and red onions.

"Stans" at the Old House

The newest addition to the restaurant and grounds is the small heritage house Mike had moved to the property. Now fully remodeled and surrounded by flowers and herb gardens, "Stans" retails Old House products, such as fresh baked breads and pastries, jams, jellies, vinegars and sauces. The fresh pasta, salads and complete take-home meals are impossible to resist. However, be sure to leave room for the incredible homemade chocolates.

Getting There

From Nanaimo, drive north on Highway 19. Entering Courtenay, turn right on 17th Street. Before crossing the bridge, turn right again on Riverside. The Old House is just ahead on your left.

The Old House is surrounded by beautiful gardens and faces the river.

■ APRIL POINT LODGE

Address: Box 1, Campbell River, British Columbia V9W 4Z9
Telephone: (604) 285-2222; FAX (604) 285-2411
Location: On Quadra Island, opposite the mouth of Campbell
                  River on the eastern coast of Vancouver Island
Hosts: The Petersons
Room Rates: $139 to $199 for two guests (Canadian); $50 per
                  additional guest. Children under 16 stay free. One,
                  Two-and three-bedroom suites from $395; one- to
                  six-bedroom guest houses from $395. Off-season
                  rates offer up to 50% discount.
Credit Cards: American Express, Diners Club, MasterCard, Visa
Remarks: All meals à la carte except packages. High season
                  June through September.

April Point Lodge is a world-class resort that is sited on some 3.5 miles of shoreline on Quadra Island. Over 200 acres of coastal forest surround the main lodge and its guest cabins. The lodge was founded by Phil and Phyllis Peterson in 1944 and is still run by Phyllis, Eric and Warren Peterson. Today's refined lodge emerged from seven local fisherman's beach shacks built on what was then known as Poverty Point.

The handsome main lodge is the gathering place, it includes the dining room, Oyster Bar, Fireside Lounge, conference rooms, office, and guest rooms. Suites within the lodge feature living rooms with fireplaces and sun decks overlooking the swimming pool and Inside Passage to Alaska. April Point's lodgings all offer views of either the bay or the passage. Many include fireplaces, jacuzzi baths, kitchenettes and hot tubs.

■ Total Fishing

All year around, the nurturing waters of Discovery Passage are obliging host to tens of thousands of schools of salmon. Early season offers blueback or immature coho salmon, which gain as much as a pound a week all season. By August these coho will weigh up to 10 pounds and they are followed by the Northern coho that will weigh as much as 25 pounds and may be caught on Bucktail flies in September and October. Chinook, King or Spring are all names for the same biggest salmon, which are here all year, but the favorite times to fish for them are from May to October. July and August you can catch "springs" up to 60 pounds.

April Point Lodge maintains the a fleet of Boston Whalers from 15 to 25 feet in length. These swift boats are manned by the lodge guides

and will carry you from the lodge dock into the abundant waters of the passage. Fifty highly experienced guides help make the fishing fun and fruitful. With strong hands-on experience, and a thorough development program at the lodge, these guides rank among the most respected in British Columbia. In addition to vast knowledge of fishing techniques, they are well versed in local history, native fishing methods and food preparation, safety, and marine life management and conservation.

Generally, guides fish with the guests for the duration of their stay. Guided trips cost $55 to $75 per hour for two guests with a four-hour minimum. Cost includes the boat, guide, tackle, fuel and bait. It is customary to tip the guide, either daily or at the end of your stay. The week's catch may be frozen and packaged for travel, or you may have it smoked, canned or made into lachs.

Fresh Air Appetites

A day of fishing, or just breathing the fresh saltwater air, builds a healthy appetite. Fortunately, the lodge prides itself on quality dining. The fresh seafood selections are naturally extensive and change daily depending on local catches. A livewell built into the deck outside the dining room holds live Dungeness crabs, Nova Scotia lobster, as well as prawns, shrimp, cod and the occasional octopus. Should you choose, the kitchen will prepare your very own catch and serve it to you in the dining room. Menu items also include fresh island Rack of lamb, prime rib with Yorkshire pudding. Eric cooks dinner on his outdoor barbecue, twice a week. Some of our favorite selections are the Alder smoked salmon, the barbecued rack of Lamb Alexis or the wonderful Drunken Crab. Lunches are a delight with Chef Andrew Bose in attendance. The Petersons have a farm on the south end of the island where they grow produce, herbs and organic vegetables for the lodge. Phyllis still supervises the making of home-made pies, muffins and the renowned "Mrs. P's" Stickie Buns.

The dining room, with its superb collection of Northwest Coast Indian masks, set among massive cedar beams, overlooks Discovery Passage. At night, the passage is an endless procession of lights with passing ships, tugs and fishing boats. During the day you can watch seals, whales, sea lions and eagles. Guests gather in the Fireside Bar before dinner to swap fishing tales and the adventure of the day, be it feeding eagles or seeing Killer Whales.

Beside The Point

Quadra Island boasts a strong Indian heritage that bears exploration. A Kwakiutl Indian village is near the lodge and has a fascinating historical museum. At Cape Mudge, the working lighthouse and ancient

The lodge has a variety of waterfront rooms and suites.

petroglyph sites are well worth the visit. Beachcombing, clam digging, oyster picking, and hiking are accessible from the lodge. Boating picnics may also be arranged. For a real surprise, ask about "swimming with the salmon" in the Campbell River. I guarantee, you'll never have a better adventure. Helifishing and "flightseeing" are also exciting ways to explore the area, from West Coast beaches to Vancouver Island's highest peaks.

Getting There

By car, from Vancouver or Seattle, take the Tsawwassen or Horseshoe Bay ferry to Nanaimo; go north to Campbell River. Take the Quadra Island ferry. Follow Pidcock Road to the lodge. To fly, scheduled air service is available from Vancouver to Campbell River, where you can take April Point's water taxi or limousine service to the lodge. From Sea-Tac Airport in Seattle, you can make arrangements with float plane services to pick you up at the airport and drive you to downtown Seattle, where their float planes are moored. From there it's a two-hour flight directly to the lodge.

DURLACHER HOF

Address:	Box 1125, 7055 Nesters Road, Whistler, British Columbia V0N 1B0
Telephone:	(604) 932-1924; FAX (604) 938-1980
Location:	One mile north of Whistler Village, 75 miles north of Vancouver
Hosts:	Erika and Peter Durlacher, Owners/Innkeepers
Room Rates:	Winter: $99 to $169 (Canadian) per room, double occupancy; five- and seven-day ski packages from $499. Summer: $79 to $129 per person; three-day summer packages from $149 per person. Includes full breakfast.
Credit Cards:	MasterCard, Visa
Remarks:	Two-night minimum on weekends, three nights on holiday weekends, seven nights during Christmas vacation. Handicapped accessible. No smoking. No pets. Not appropriate for children. Honeymoon package available. German is also spoken.

Only a short hop from the two highest alpine skiing mountains in North America is a quaint pension built in traditional Austrian fashion. Originally from Austria themselves, Erika and Peter Durlacher have designed and decorated their Durlacher Hof after the farmhouses that dot their native Alps. Every detail is authentic, from edelweiss in bloom to the farmhouse kachelofen (fireplace/oven). In fact, the Los Angeles Times wrote, it's "difficult to tell whether you're in Innsbruck, St. Anton or Lech."

Whistler Village has become one of the most popular year-round mountain resorts on the Pacific coast. Known best for its alpine skiing, the resort is home to Whistler and Blackcomb mountains, impressive peaks that boast record vertical drops of 5,280 feet and 5,020 feet, respectively. Come summer, Whistler Village becomes a fair-weather outdoor lover's paradise.

Personal Slippers

Since 1988, when the Durlacher Hof opened, the bed-and-breakfast has practiced a typically European tradition. A tidy basket of slippers, conveniently located in the entry, awaits each new arrival. As you enter the hof, you are asked to kick off your shoes and don one of the Durlacher's alternatives. Your new slippers are then yours to wear for the remainder of your stay. This clever custom is just one example of the comfortable, homey atmosphere that owner and innkeeper Erika Durlacher creates naturally. Erika, complete with her Austrian accent and a will to pamper, puts all of her energies into her

guests. She works individually with each guest, seeing to it that you get the most out of your trip to Whistler.

A Touch of the Tyrol

The spacious Durlacher Hof offers just seven guest rooms, each named for a mountain in the Austrian Alps. As we expected, the guest rooms are warm and welcoming with hand-carved pine furniture, and extra-long queen and twin beds. The beds are draped with thick goose down duvets and pillows. Private baths offer hot showers or soothing Jacuzzi tubs, ideal after a full day of skiing or golfing. Most of the guest rooms have a balcony, complete with superb views of Whistler, Blackcomb or Wedge Mountain.

A charming European styled guest lounge with wood floors, hand-crafted furnishings, and cushion wing chairs provides cozy warmth and fellowship in the evenings. An inviting brick patio with umbrellaed wooden tables make a perfect spot for morning coffee, afternoon tea, or a few chapters worth of that best-seller you've been meaning to pick up.

The Durlachers have also included a sauna, a roomy outdoor whirlpool and badminton court, not to mention ski storage and daily maid service and ample free parking.

Austrian Cuisine

Before slipping out to the slopes, guests enjoy a bountiful old country breakfast with hot coffee and tea, fruit juices, home-baked breads and European specialties. Afternoon tea with goodies is also served, for those who stay behind or come in early. On special occasions, the Durlacher Hof serves dinner for its guests, featuring the mouth-watering works of guest chefs or Erika's own pork roasts with spatzle, robust dumpling soups, linzer torte and strudel. On request, Erika has been known to serve outstanding five-course dinners fit for a king. Beer, wine and liquors to complement the European cuisine are available.

The alpine setting and ambience of the Durlacher Hof makes it a pleasantly unusual place for a small business meeting or retreat. The conference room will accommodate up to 20 people and has available catering services, a FAX machine and secretarial services.

Summer and Winter Sports Alike

Some say Whistler offers skiers the most exciting high alpine experience on the continent. You be the judge; you have 100+ runs on Whistler Mountain and the same on Blackcomb to choose from.

Full breakfasts are enjoyed before heading out to experience Whistler.

With an average snowfall of 28 feet, there is lots of opportunity for snowshoeing, cross-country skiing, sleigh rides and snowmobiling. Summer and fall in Whistler are beautiful and breathtaking in a whole different way. Green alpine meadows, colorful wildflowers and azure mountain lakes offer the best in sailing, fishing, hiking, horseback riding, even para-gliding. If golf is your game, play the Arnold Palmer championship course, or the new John Trent course at the club, named by *Golf Magazine* as one of the best golf resorts in the world. Erika can keep you informed about the schedule of classical, jazz and bluegrass music festivals throughout the season.

Getting There

From Vancouver, travel 75 miles (125 km) north on Highway 99 into Whistler. After the third traffic light in Whistler, take the first left, which is Nesters Road. The Durlacher Hof will be on your immediate left. Transportation to the inn from the Vancouver International Airport may be arranged via bus, helicopter, rental car or train.

PARK ROYAL HOTEL

Address:	540 Clyde Avenue, West Vancouver, British Columbia, V7T 2J7
Telephone:	(604) 926-5511; FAX (604) 926-6082
Location:	In West Vancouver, just north of the Lion's Gate Bridge
Host:	Mario Corsi, Owner/ Manager
Room Rates:	$95 to $225 (Canadian)
Credit Cards:	American Express, Carte Blanche, Diners Club, En Route, MasterCard, Visa
Remarks:	Coffee or tea and morning newspaper delivered to room, complimentary. Free parking.

"The Park Royal is a country style inn found in a busy metropolis," says host Mario Corsi. "It's cozy, and has a staff who really cares about the comfort of the guests." Mario should know; after all, most of his staff have been with him for a good part of his 20 years as manager of the hotel. Mario's European upbringing and hotel training have led him to create a high standard of service and quality reminiscent of a Continental hotel. "Nothing phony or glitzy," he says proudly. "Just a good feeling, like being in a little village." That philosophy and Mario's enthusiasm are what make the Park Royal such a rare find.

On The River Bank

Located on the north side of Vancouver's harbor, just minutes from the bustling downtown area, the Tudor style, ivy festooned hotel provides a quiet retreat for the business or vacation traveler. The two-story building is surrounded by trimmed lawns and flower beds. The Capilano River flows along the back. Twelve of the inn's 30 rooms face the river and overlook the gardens. On quiet nights you can open the window and be lulled to sleep by the sounds of rushing water. Most rooms offer queen or double beds; a few have twins. All rooms have private baths, and are individually decorated with floral print wallpapers, antique oak furniture and leaded glass windows. A large suite offers a jacuzzi, VCR, plush terry robes and a wet bar. The morning newspaper and coffee or tea are delivered to your room upon request. These are just a few of the touches that lend Park Royal its intimacy.

Plans are under way to upgrade and remodel some of the older rooms. The quietest rooms are on the water side, so if that is a concern, ask for the second floor, riverside rooms.

A Lively Pub

An authentic English pub downstairs offers lively piano entertainment Monday through Saturday evenings. Michael, the piano player, has been playing at the pub for years despite his youth, and is rarely ever stumped when you call out a request. The Corsi touch is felt here, too, with Angelica Corsi often found overseeing the pub atmosphere, bar and pub food selections.

Public rooms are paneled in dark woods. Flowered and scenic print draperies hang on the windows. We have spent many a winter evening in front of the big stone fireplace, warmed by the crackling fire, enjoying the music and eating the great homemade potato chips. A note of caution, most Canadian pubs do not have a separate "no smoking" area, so be forewarned.

Dining In Style

Park Royal is as proud of its restaurant as it is of its rooms. The Tudor Room is regarded as one of the top dining spots in the city. One of the sure signs this acclaim is real is that the room is often full of locals. Regional specialties and old standards combine to create a diverse menu. Hans Schaub, chef here for 18 years, is quite proud of the freshness and consistency of his menu. The dining room overlooks the garden, and is warmly appointed with tapestry-covered chairs, vintage prints and stained glass. Dinner entrees include breast of pheasant with red currants and brandy, black pasta with smoked salmon, red caviar and cream, and traditional favorites such as beef Wellington and Chateaubriand. A resident baker supplies fresh breads and stunning desserts.

Breakfast and lunch selections are as noteworthy as dinner. Begin the day with huevos rancheros or "Eggs Park Royal" (poached eggs, smoked salmon, salmon caviar and Hollandaise sauce). Lunch offers a steak and kidney pie, scallops in a fresh basil cream, or veal scaloppine. Herbs from the inn's greenhouse are used in the cuisine, giving a bright, fresh taste. In warm weather, lunch, cocktails and snacks may be taken on the secluded patio off the dining room.

The Park Royal has several second story conference rooms. The attendees are served meals and hors d' oeuvres directly from the Tudor Room kitchen.

Exploring the "Other" Vancouvers

Park Royal is located in West Vancouver, just a few minutes walk from the Park Royal Shopping Center. Over 190 shops are found in this trendy mall, including three of Canada's top department stores - The Bay, Eaton's and Woodward's. Ambleside Park stretches along

The Tudor Dining Room looks on to the gardens and Capilano River.

the shore behind the mall and may be reached by following a trail outside the Park Royal Hotel.

North Vancouver offers additional opportunities for exploration. Grouse Mountain is a favorite destination of ours in any season. Two aerial tramways depart for the mountain top every 15 minutes, offering spectacular views of the city and environs. En route to the mountain, walk the Capilano Suspension Bridge. Constructed of wire rope with wood decking, the bridge stretches 450 feet across the canyon, some 230 feet above the river.

Getting There

Follow Georgia Street through Vancouver and cross the Lion's Gate Bridge. Take the West Vancouver Exit and turn right on Taylor Way, then right onto Clyde Avenue. Go one block, turn right. The hotel is on the left. From Trans-Canada 1, turn off at Exit 13 (Taylor Way Vancouver), go downhill to Clyde Avenue and turn left at the Park Royal sign.

CORSI TRATTORIA

Address:	1 Lonsdale, North Vancouver, British Columbia V7M 2E4
Telephone:	(604) 987-9910
Location:	Near Lonsdale Quay Market in Vancouver Harbour
Hosts:	Antonio and Edy Corsi
Cuisine:	Italian
Prices:	Entrees $10.95 to $16.95 (Canadian)
Credit Cards:	American Express, Diners Club, MasterCard, Visa
Hours:	Lunch 12 p.m. to 2:30 p.m. , Monday through Friday - no lunch on weekends. Dinner 5 p.m. to 10:30 p.m. Monday through Sunday.
Remarks:	Reservations recommended.

Corsi Trattoria, located on North Vancouver's waterfront across from the Lonsdale Quay Market and the SeaBus to downtown Vancouver, offers Italian cuisine in an authentic Mediterranean atmosphere. A bright green awning outside yields to the white stucco and terra cotta inside. Burgundy and pink linens, candles and photographs lend a cozy feeling. "You can go in blue jeans or a long gown," says co-owner Antonio Corsi.

The Corsi brothers, Mario and Antonio, have been in the restaurant and hotel business since their childhood, when their family ran a small hotel outside Rome. "It's not just our business," Mario says,"it's our life."

Both brothers are involved in the restaurant and Antonio is chef. "He is always in and out of the kitchen talking to guests," says his wife, Edy. "It's simple, the way a trattoria should be," adds Antonio. "We put our effort into the food, service and atmosphere and work at making everyone feel at home." Apparently their efforts are successful. Recently the Italian government honored the Corsi family for its exceptional efforts.

A Classic

Corsi Trattoria blends the finest of central Italian cuisine with the freshest of West Coast ingredients. The restaurant orders its veal from a special source in Montreal. Fish and fowl are carefully selected from local markets.

Classic dishes include a wide variety of antipasto as well as over 50 pasta specialties. Fettuccine, gnocchetti, spaghetti, fusilli, bucatini and capelli d'angelo are among the pastas made fresh daily on the premises. Featured entrees are penne all'Arrabiata (spicy tomato sauce with bacon and Romano cheese), and spinach fettucine with cream, ham and mushrooms.

Though Corsi Trattoria is noted for its pasta dishes, the menu extends far beyond. Non-pasta dishes include prawns, pan fried in butter and sprinkled with oregano and white vermouth, or a veal scaloppine in an apple and cream sauce. Accompanying vegetables arrive perfectly al dente on side plates. Dinner salads include spinach and mushroom, mixed greens or fresh mozzarella and tomato.The most popular item on the menu is a feast of five different pastas in an array of sauces (minimum of two orders). "L'Abbuffata" includes four different pastas, a mixed salad, lamb, veal piccata, prawns, zabaglione and espresso (also a minimum of two orders).

For dessert, creme caramel, zabaglione and zuccotto (an Italian chocolate cake) are a few of the options. An almost entirely Italian wine list offers selections in many price ranges.

Getting There

Once in North Vancouver, go east on Marine Drive to Lonsdale. Turn right. The restaurant is located on the last right corner.

Some of the selections are marker "For Italians only."

TEAHOUSE RESTAURANT

Address:	Ferguson Point in Stanley Park
Telephone:	(604) 669-3281
Location:	On the most westerly point of Stanley Park, over-looking the ocean.
Hosts:	Felix Zurbuchen, General Manager; Maria Manalastas and Simon Levin, Managers
Cuisine:	Country French
Prices:	Brunch entrées $8.95 to $14.95; Lunch entrées $8.95 to $13.95; dinner entrées $11.95 to $19.95 (Canadian)
Credit Cards:	American Express, MasterCard, Visa
Hours:	Lunch 11:30 a.m. to 2:30 p.m. Monday - Friday; Dinner 5:30 p.m. to closing daily; Saturday brunch 11:30 a.m. to 2:30 p.m.; Sunday brunch 10:30 a.m. to 2:30 p.m. Open daily except Christmas Day.

Situated in the midst of Stanley Park (rated one of the world's finest parks-within-a-city by *National Geographic Magazine*), the Teahouse combines elegance and nature in a most comfortable way. A recent poll named the Teahouse the most romantic restaurant in Vancouver.

Ferguson Point was a military installation during World War II, and the present-day Teahouse served as a garrison and officers' mess. In 1978, present owner and Vancouver native, Brent Davies,leased the house from the Parks Board, renovated and opened it as a restaurant. So your not misled, the name was kept for historical purposes. The Teahouse does not serve high tea in the afternoon, but does serve lunch and dinner throughout the week and a not-to-be-missed weekend brunch.

A Garden Within A Garden

Facing the front of the restaurant, you'll see the glass-enclosed "greenhouse" environment, which Brent added to the original structure. Brent calls this is "the Conservatory." Inside, trees reach to the sky under a glass roof, which warms the room in the winter and keeps you cool under the summer sun. On the opposite side of the restaurant is the Drawing Room. This is a more intimate setting but also has walls of windows and a large tree growing in the center of the room. This is the place we love to linger over a really decadent dinner and a bottle of wine from the cellar reserve list.

The Teahouse Restaurant serves weekend brunches as well as daily lunches and dinners. The cuisine far surpasses the connotation of a "teahouse," and rarely do you find a staff with the degree of professionalism and friendliness that characterizes the people who work here. Ask for their recommendation on wine to accompany your appetizer of grilled goat cheese with almonds and baby greens in raspberry dressing. Yellow fin tuna tartar with capers, red onions, chives and an anchovy dressing may require another selection. As an entrée, consider grilled salmon with a butter of 21 different ingredients, or chicken breast with Parmesan and polenta cakes in a fresh basil and pine nut sauce.

Dinner's menu is an expanded version of the luncheon menu, with specialty items such as rack of lamb, roast duck, veal, venison, salmon, prawns, scallops and fresh fish of the day. The Teahouse offers a truly international selection of wines on three individual wine lists to complement your meal.

Getting There

From north and west Vancouver, take the Lion's Gate Bridge. Immediately after the bridge, take the Prospect Point/Park Drive Exit for two kilometers (1.5 miles) to the restaurant at Ferguson Point. From downtown Vancouver, take Georgia Street to the same exit.

A recent poll named the Teahouse the most romantic restaurant in Vancouver.

SEASONS IN THE PARK RESTAURANT

Address: In Queen Elizabeth Park at 33th and Cambie Street
Telephone: (604) 874-8008
Location: On Little Mountain in Queen Elizabeth Park
Hosts: Richard Baker, General Manager; Megan Buckley and Brent Hayman, Managers
Cuisine: Pacific Northwest
Prices: Brunch entrées $8.95 to $13.95; lunch entrées $8.95 to$13.95; dinner entrées $11.95 to $19.95 (Canadian)
Credit Cards: American Express, MasterCard, Visa
Hours: Lunch 11:30 a.m. to 2:30 p.m. Monday - Friday; Dinner 5:30 p.m. ; Saturday brunch 11:30 a.m. to 2:30 p.m.; Sunday brunch 10:30 a.m. to 2:30 p.m.

Queen Elizabeth Park is set on Little Mountain and affords the most phenomenal view of Vancouver. From Seasons in the Park, you can see Grouse Mountain, Vancouver Island and the city skyline. Even most local people don't know how wonderful the view is from here. We believe this is the best view site in the entire area.

A Room With A View

The main dining room features wall-to-wall windows and tiered seating from front to back so that your view won't be obstructed. The Gazebo, built onto the main structure, is situated at the edge of what used to be a deep quarry. Flowering shrubs and gardens are etched into the hillsides of the quarry.

Lunch at Seasons in the Park begins with appetizers, including a roast prawn salad with garden greens, sweet peppers, avocado and mango pepper dressing, or Pacific oyster stew, with freshly shucked gold mantle oysters lightly cooked with leeks and cream. Seasonal soups and a choice of salad entrées complement a full selection of main course items including smoked black Alaska cod poached in milk and served with a light mustard dill sauce, or farfalle tossed with pesto and artichoke hearts and sundried tomatoes.

For a complete romantic evening, arrive early enough to watch the sun set behind the mountains and the lights of the city begin to sparkle. Start your dinner with cold peppered salmon poached in a terrine with Chardonnay and a trio of peppercorns with a dill dressing. This will lead nicely into your entrée, whether it's Atlantic scallops with Quady Elysium, seared with the Elysium and served over winter greens, or glazed pork rib chop, pan roasted on the bone and glazed with sage and served with an apple-onion relish.

A Wine List To Remember

Seasons in the Park's wine selection is the same outstanding list you'll find at the Teahouse. Three separate lists include a full range of international wines (and we do mean "full;" Argentina, New Zealand and Greece are included in the standard wine offering, as well as the more familiar European and West Coast selections). A fine cellar reserve list and ever-changing wine-by-the-glass feature sheet are readily available.

All of Seasons' desserts are prepared on the premises. For a light finish, try a trio of sorbets - three seasonal fruit sherbets with fresh fruits and almond lace wafer.

Getting There

From downtown Vancouver, go south on Cambie Street to 33rd Avenue. Turn left at the stop sign and follow the road and signs that indicate the way to the restaurant. It's at the top of Little Mountain.

Dine over looking the Vancouver skyline and the Grouse Mountain.

HATHEUME LAKE RESORT

Address:	P.O. Box 490, Peachland, British Columbia V0H1X0
Telephone:	(604) 767-2642
Location:	About one-half hour by unpaved road from the Sunset Main Road Exit on Highway 97C in central British Columbia
Hosts:	Tim and Janet Tullis, Gus and Leni Averill
Room Rates:	$195 to $215 per day (Canadian); American plan; children 5-12 pay two-thirds rate.
Credit Cards:	None
Remarks:	Reservations necessary.

Over the years, as trails and roads sliced farther into the interior of British Columbia, fishermen discovered a remote pocket of lakes known to native Indians as Hatheume, or "Big Fish." Of all freshwater game fish, none holds quite the reputation for size and fighting spirit as the Kamloops trout, a hardy strain of rainbow. They are found almost exclusively in the isolated lakes that dot the forested Nicola Plateau, situated between the Coastal Range and the Canadian Rockies. Our first visit to Hatheume convinced us that, if you are seeking peace and quiet in a remote setting, Hatheume Lake Resort is an excellent choice.

A Wilderness Retreat

Among the straight pine and quaking aspen along the shore of Hatheume Lake, you will find a splendid lodge and six comfortable cabins, all built of handhewn logs. For a few days, or a week, you can become part of the exhilarating freshness of this rare wilderness. Each of the eight lakes that are fished by resort guests still support resident loons, osprey, eagles, deer, bear and moose.

The exuberant greeting from Gus Averill and wife, Leni, is as genuine as the trout jumping out there in the lake. Then again, it may be Tim Tullis or his wife, Janet, who come from the dock to welcome you. That bottle of Okanagan wine in your cabin is just one of the ways they have of saying they're glad you've made it. Until the moment you leave, they and their very competent staff will do everything they can to make sure you're comfortable and content. The Averills and Tullis's have plenty to do just keeping the equipment running and the meals coming, but they always seem to find time to give a fly casting lesson, brew a fresh pot of coffee or suggest spots for photography.

The facilities at Hatheume are basic—clean and homey. Each of the well-heated cabins has two large carpeted bedrooms with extra-long twin beds, a private bath with shower and a nicely furnished sitting room that has a panoramic view of the lake. The cabins are arranged to assure privacy; you can sit on your covered porch and see nothing but the water, hear nothing but the call of the loons. In the lodge, surrounded by renderings of area wildlife by prominent B.C. artists, you can prop your feet on the raised hearth of the huge circular fireplace and read or chat or nap.

The Mornings

Each morning, Tim or Gus delivers freshly brewed coffee or tea to your cabin—something we especially appreciate, since it ensures we make it to breakfast. Janet and Leni prepare tasty and varied meals, served ranch-style. Over sausages, hotcakes, hashbrowns and homemade muffins or rolls, everyone decides on the day's fishing spot. Large lunches are already packed. Four-wheel drive vehicles are ready for you to drive the back roads through jack pine forests and high plateau meadows, where wildflowers abound, to the outlying lakes. There you will find sturdy wooden boats equipped with outboard motors, boat cushions, anchors, nets and tackle boxes. If you prefer even more adventure, the lodge also provides float tubes and other accessories. We usually choose a different lake each day and the wonderful thing is that we are the only ones there.

Cooperative Trout

The eight lakes provide plenty of variety and are accessible only to guests of the resort. Jenny and Rouse lakes are the most remote, perhaps the most scenic, and often yield the most fish. Fishing is consistently good. Because of the abundance of feed in these cold, spring-fed lakes, the trout commonly reach one to three pounds, and there's always a chance you'll catch a trophy fish. The fish aren't finicky, either; just about any fishing method results in a good catch.

Seldom do non-fishermen feel left out; guests can follow their own paths, content with the absence of pressure or responsibility. Hatheume has a fleet of mountain bikes available for working off those hefty meals, or try our favorite game, target golf off the dock using floating golf balls.

At the end of the day, guests gather together again for dinner. It might be ribs or roast, veal cutlets or turkey served with heaping plates of fresh vegetables and freshly baked rolls. Everything, including dessert, is as hearty as it is delicious. Evenings are peaceful and sleep comes easily.

This is a destination resort, so a holiday here requires thoughtful planning. Write early, ask questions, make your reservations and be

The Main Lodge and the cabins face Hatheume Lake.

sure to inquire about their special schools: fly fishing or gourmet cooking. Remember that even during the hot summer months, the temperature at this altitude (4,600 feet) can be brisk at night. Come prepared for the odd rain storm. Most guests return again and again; they can depend on the hosts to be as cooperative as the fish. When your stay has ended, you may be reticent about packing your gear and starting your car again. Just take your fish (which can be smoked or vacuum packed for your convenience), your photos and your memories, and begin thinking about next year.

Getting There

From Vancouver, take Highway 1 eastward to Hope, then take the toll Coquihalla Highway 5 north toward Merritt. Just prior to Merritt, take Exit 286 (97C Kelowna). Take the Sunset Main Road Exit, turn right, then turn left onto a gravel road 5 km (3 mi) through underpass. Continue 15 km (9 mi) to lodge. Or travel Highway 97 to Peachland. Six km (4 mi) north on Peachland of 97, take 97C west toward Merritt. Take Sunset Main Road Exit and follow the directions above.

EMERALD LAKE LODGE

Address: P.O. Box 10, Field, British Columbia V0A 1G0
Telephone: (604) 343-6321; toll free (800) 663-6336, reservations only
Location: On the shore of Emerald Lake, one hour from Banff
Hosts: Tom Bornhorst, Manager; Pat and Connie O'Connor, Proprietors
Room Rates: Superior rooms: $100 to $220. Deluxe rooms: $125 to $260. Executive suites: $150 to $285. (Canadian)
Credit Cards: American Express, EnRoute, MasterCard, Visa
Remarks: Children under 12 free with parents. No pets.

When he first spotted the lake, Tom Wilson knew he'd made a mistake, and an embarrassing one at that. As a guide working for the railroad in the late 1800s, Tom had come upon many an undiscovered lake and had aptly named them. But this one was extraordinary. Encircled by a forest of giant pines, it had water as pure and tranquil as fine glacial silt, as sparkling green as an emerald. Emeralds! Emerald Lake.

But there already was an Emerald Lake. Tom had named it himself not long before. That had been a pretty lake, but nothing compared to this. "Perhaps Louise would fancy a lake being named after her," he thought.

Creme de la Creme

Built by the Canadian Pacific Railway in 1902 as one of a series of bungalow camps erected to encourage travel and thus recoup the cost of the expensive rail line, the Emerald Lake Chalet was the creme de la creme. The majestic lodge of handhewn timber and massive stone fireplaces offered the very latest in modern conveniences—electricity, wood stoves and hardwood floors. The rate, even with the added amenity of a full orchestra to entertain the guests, was still exorbitant—$5 per day. The chalet became the private retreat only of the adventurous of spirit and the affluent.

Calgary resident Pat O'Connor had watched the sun set on the grandeur of the Emerald Lake Chalet many times. He was concerned over the steady decline of the chalet. In 1980 Pat purchased the chalet and its surrounding 13 acres, beginning a process, he recalls, that "I would never have dreamed could be so difficult." The property, which was and continues to be under the scrutiny of Park Canada, took six years to restore.

The $8.5 million renovation that produced the new Emerald Lake Lodge reflects O'Connors respect for the delicate balance between commercial and environmental concerns. To insure the peaceful quiet of the site, the parking lot is located five minutes away from the lodge. Guests unload, park their cars and are quickly delivered to the lodge by shuttle. The lodge's 24 new buildings were built 25 feet off the ground so that the surrounding vegetation would be able to regenerate. The 85 guest units spread over three hillsides. The studios and the suites contain queen-sized beds covered with comforters, and the homey feel of antiques and wicker. All rooms have stone hearth fireplaces (and an on-call woodsman to light it for you), private entrances, full baths and telephones. You won't find televisions, radios or clocks to distract you here.

The property is on the tip of a finger of land that reaches into the lake, leaving water on three sides. It is reachable only by crossing a wooden bridge. Pat and his crew restored the 15,000-square-foot chalet to its rustic grandeur. The building's two massive stone fireplaces remain the focal point for the Emerald Lounge and lobby. And the Kicking Horse Bar's 1882 oak bar adds a grand reminder of the Yukon's lively Gold Rush days.

An old-fashioned veranda shades the dining room's spectacular views. Elegant in chintzes of dusty rose, gray and hunter green, the rustic room has a comfortable coziness. And the menu's mountain cuisine successfully pleases nouvelle palates, as well as those that prefer simpler fare. But whatever your choice, leave room for dessert. The Chocolatissimo and Black Forest cakes and the cheesecakes are as spectacular as the lake itself.

Combining Business and Pleasure

An ideal location for board meetings, workshops and classroom-style seminars for 10 to 100, Emerald Lake Lodge offers seven conference areas and a full spectrum of audio visual equipment. The lodge is especially suited to occasions such as weddings and anniversaries. Honeymoon units are set at the secluded end of the property and are thoughtfully stocked with chilled champagne, a floral bouquet and basket of assorted goodies.

There's a Club House with an outdoor 14-foot hot tub, sauna and sundeck, with wonderful views down into the lake. Sitting in the warm waters of the hot tub and watching the color of the lake change at dusk is our special way of celebrating each visit to the lodge.

Spirit of the Canadian Rockies

"Were looking for people who want to spend time in the mountains, for people who want all the advantages of the Rockies without roughing it," says Pat. Emerald Lake Lodge does its best to fulfill the

The hot tub has stunning views down into Emerald Lake and up to the mountains.

promise of the great outdoors. The tour desk has information on such seasonal activities as horseback riding, canoeing, fishing, white-water rafting and great spots for sightseeing. For ambitious hikers who want to wander in the surrounding ranges, the lodge staff can arrange overnight stays at hiking huts. Burgess fossil beds, is a strenuous but rewarding two-hour hike. Takkakkaw Falls, the third highest waterfall in Canada, is easily reachable by car.

In the winter, you can ski the way the Canadians prefer, from helicopter. The area has some of the best heli-skiing in the world. For cross-country enthusiasts, there are 50 miles of trails where deer, elk and other wildlife roam.

Getting There

From Calgary, take the Trans-Canada Highway 1 west past Banff and north past Lake Louise. Go down the pass to Field, B.C. Follow the signs for Natural Bridges and Emerald Lake. The parking lot for overnight guests will be on your left. Call the lodge when you arrive, for a shuttle.

BUFFALO MOUNTAIN LODGE

Address: P.O. Box 1326, Banff, Alberta TOL 0C0
Telephone: (403) 762-2400; toll free (800) 661-1367, reservations only
Location: On Tunnel Mountain, above the town of Banff
Hosts: Paula Mattison, Manager; Pat and Connie O'Connor, Proprietors
Room Rates: Deluxe and studio suites: $95 to $170. One-bedroom loft and two-bedroom chalets: $135 to $185. (Canadian)
Credit Cards: American Express, En Route, MasterCard, Visa
Remarks: Children under 12 stay free with parents. No pets.

Blackfoot Indian legends describe the area known today as Tunnel Mountain, overlooking scenic, historic Banff. Bordered by the granite spires of Cascade Mountain and Mount Rundle, rock formations called hoodoos rose out of the sweeping Bow Valley, where moose, elk, deer and bison were plentiful. Here the earth's hot mineral baths provided rejuvenation. It was a peaceful life for the Indians and still is for visitors to this scenic part of Canada.

Respect For The Past

With a spirit of veneration for the past, for unspoiled nature and life's simple pleasures, Pat O'Connor and his wife, Connie, have blended their talents to create Buffalo Mountain Lodge. Above the town of Banff, the lodge's forested setting offers seclusion, privacy and pure mountain air. It's the kind of place that compels you to slow down.

"We were drawing from the past for things built properly and built with heart," says Witold Twardowski, the creative director of the lodge. The love and craftsmanship that went into the main lodge's handhewn construction is evident. High, open-beamed ceilings display a massive stone fireplace and the custom-made cherry, pine and bent-willow furnishings are beautifully accented with copper. The simple elegance of the lodge's design extends to the custom cherry and pine furnishings of the dining room.

The lodge's chefs, taking pride in using only the freshest ingredients, present delicious menus that feature hearty soups and breads, superb entrees and freshly baked pastries and desserts. In the summer, you can sample the cuisine from the shade of a patio table, or, at any time, enjoy breakfast in bed.

Canadian Hospitality

The 85 townhouse units spread across the property can accommodate up to 250 guests in two- and four-unit condominium-style buildings. You have the option of choosing from a deluxe unit with one queen bed or two double beds, or, for larger families, a two-bedroom chalet that can sleep six and includes a full kitchen.

Throughout the units, the warm, rich tones of custom pine, antique and wicker furnishings are accented with splashes of turquoise and fresh floral arrangements. Most units included a stone fireplace and private balcony and all provide telephones, cable television and other personal touches. There are a variety of room layouts and styles, enabling you to specify your choice.

True to its heritage as a native gathering place, Buffalo Mountain Lodge is also a splendid meeting place. Two well-appointed conference rooms can accommodate from 10 to 100 people for seminars, workshops and retreats. The Strathcona Room features a balcony with a breathtaking view of Cascade Mountain. The Wainwright Room has a landscaped outdoor patio.

The lodge's cheerful staff go out of their way to pamper and please. Guests have access to the property's outdoor spa facilities, which include an oversized 14-foot hot tub and steam room. A seasonal program of activities is available. Manager Paula Mattison has been with the lodge for several years and has developed a very able staff, so you will receive lots of willing assistance in coordinating your wedding, dinner party or family reunion.

Tradition of a Rocky Mountain Holiday

No matter the season, Buffalo Mountain Lodge offers outdoor activities by day and the luxury of an alpine resort by night. Banff, known the world over for its beauty and soothing hot mineral springs, provides the perfect base camp for exploring the outlying areas. We appreciate the quiet found at the lodge, yet its easy access to the more urban activities of Banff.

You can explore hiking trails by foot or by horseback, canoe or kayak down the beautiful Bow River. There's great golf at nearby Banff Springs, and the lodge can provide picnic lunches for a day of fishing at Lake Minnewanka.

For winter guests, there's the snow. Everyone's heard of the featherlight powder of the Canadian Rockies. With Banff's central location, you are close to four world-class ski mountains — Lake Louise, Mount Norquay, Sunshine and Nakiska. The downhill skiing is fabulous and if that isn't your fancy, you can take off on a pair of cross-country skis to experience the thrill of untracked powder. A

The lodge is on Tunnel Mountain above the town of Banff.

variety of exciting ski packages, including heli-skiing, are available through the lodge and if apres-ski night life is on your list, just stop off in Banff.

Banff is also recognized for the excellence of Banff Centre's music, theatre and dance performances. The town tempts you with little boutiques, galleries and cafes. The Whyte Museum of the Canadian Rockies and the Luxton Museum do an outstanding job of reproducing the colorful history of Banff National Park and its native people. We believe Banff is best appreciated during the less crowded months. The fall and spring are ideal times to visit without the crowds associated with the busier summer and winter seasons.

Getting There

Buffalo Mountain Lodge is located on Tunnel Mountain Road just off the Trans-Canada Highway. The Calgary International Airport is 1.5 hours away. Passenger rail and bus service is also available to Banff.

Northern
Rockies

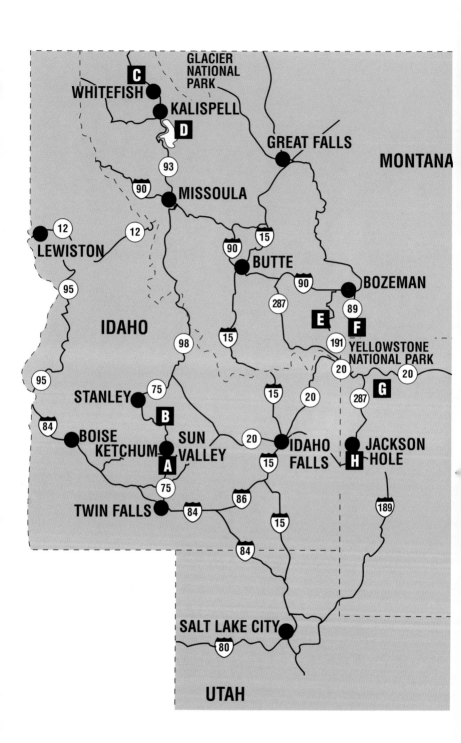

GLACIER
NATIONAL
PARK

C
WHITEFISH

KALISPELL

D

GREAT FALLS

MONTANA

93

90

MISSOULA

12

12

LEWISTON

95

90

BUTTE

15

90

BOZEMAN

287

89

IDAHO

E

F

191

YELLOWSTONE
NATIONAL PARK

98

15

20

20

95

75

STANLEY

15

20

287

G

B

20

84

BOISE

KETCHUM

SUN
VALLEY

15

IDAHO
FALLS

JACKSON
HOLE

A

H

75

86

TWIN FALLS

84

15

189

84

SALT LAKE CITY

80

UTAH

NORTHERN ROCKIES SPECIAL PLACES

A   River Street Inn

B   Idaho Rocky Mountain Ranch

C   Kandahar Lodge

D   Flathead Lake Lodge

E   Lone Mountain Ranch

F   Mountain Sky Ranch

G   Brooks Lake Lodge

H   Rusty Parrott Lodge

RIVER STREET INN

Address:	100 Rivers Street W., Ketchum, ID 83340
	P.O. Box 182, Sun Valley, ID 83353
Telephone:	(208) 726-3611
Location:	On Trail Creek in south Ketchum
Hosts:	Ginny Van Doren and Gun Taylor
Room Rates:	$100 to $150 double. Single, senior citizen, commercial and holiday rates are available.
Credit Cards:	American Express, Discover, MasterCard, Visa
Remarks:	No smoking in bedrooms.

The River Street Inn is Sun Valley's first bed and breakfast inn, and is neatly tucked on a quiet street just a few blocks from the core of Ketchum. The inn is a pleasing blend of friendly warmth and respectful privacy. Its innovative architecture weaves the charm of Victorian sensibilities with the open spaces of contemporary Western design.

In the spacious living room with sage green carpets and white-washed oak trim, comfortable couches invite you to enjoy the warmth provided by the the natural brick fireplace. From the living room, French doors open onto an expansive deck. Cottonwoods and aspens border Trail Creek, which runs below. The deck provides an ideal spot for early morning bird-watching, afternoon tea or late-night stargazing.

The nine guest rooms are really more like guest suites. Decorated in soft prints and pastels, they feature queen-sized beds, big walk-in showers, small refrigerators and our favorite amenity, Japanese soaking tubs, sized to accommodate two. Six of the suites face the Trail Creek, and three suites offer clear mountain views.

"No Rules" Rule

The intimate atmosphere of the inn was co-owner Ginny Van Doren's special goal. Years ago, Ginny left her job in San Francisco and found her heart in Sun Valley. Over the years, she worked for several restaurants in the area. Her experience led to her own success formula, one which she and assistant manager Gun Taylor share. River Street Inn's secret: let the guests set the tone. If you'd like to visit over a cup of coffee in the kitchen, the more the merrier. If you prefer privacy, it is most assuredly respected. Ginny and staff are available for friendly conversation or to help with any arrangements you may need to enhance your stay.

Breakfast at River Street Inn is an indulgent feast that will carry you well through lunchtime. Ginny's "no rules" apply here as well—

breakfast is from 8 a.m. to 10 a.m. unless you want it earlier or later, or served in your room. In the morning you can sit at the counter, looking into the open kitchen and talk with Ginny while she's preparing breakfast. Begin with fresh fruits, juices, coffee or tea. Then get ready for one of Ginny's homemade baked Danish rolls or coffeecake. Among Ginny's favorite entrees are frittatas, spinach or sausage puff pastry, or German apple pancakes.

To accommodate her many health-conscious guests, Ginny also offers low-fat substitutions, such as making pancakes with cottage cheese. If breakfast decadence is your wish, however, she can whip that up, too.

Down in the Valley

Ketchum and Sun Valley are situated in the narrow Wood River Valley. Sun Valley is most noted as a skiers' haven. Bald Mountain hovers over the town, with over 16 chairlifts and 64 runs on its 3,400 feet of vertical drop. The area offers some of the most challenging skiing in the country, yet has appeal for skiers at all levels of expertise. Sun Valley's expert staff of ski instructors is nationally acclaimed. A free shuttle runs from just across the street from River Street Inn to the base of River Run. Cross-country skiing has become increasingly popular in the area, and local outfitters will gladly arrange special backcountry trips for you.

Summer and Fall

Mardi lived for 6 years in Ketchum. She came for the skiing, but it was the summer and fall which kept her here and keep us coming back.The summer climate is warm and dry. The bright, clear days are perfect for enjoying glider rides from Hailey Airport, or golf at one of the four courses in the area. A new network of bicycle trails winds through the valley for 20 miles, and many shops in town rent mountain bikes for two-wheeled adventures. Wagon Days celebration and parade mark the end of the summer season and the look toward fall and the snows of winter. The crisp fall days are brilliantly colored by the turning of the aspen leaves, enhancing hiking and horseback riding expeditions.

North of Ketchum is a cemetery where a simple slab marks Ernest Hemingway's grave. Farther out on Trail Creek, in the heart of the country he called home, you'll find the Hemingway memorial. On it is written, "Best of all he loved the fall...the leaves yellow on the cottonwoods, leaves floating on the trout streams and above the hills the high blue windless skies."

Wood River Valley is also home to some of the best trout fishing streams in the country. Ketchum is a very friendly town, whose residents are accessible and interesting people. You can walk anywhere

All the spacious rooms have views of either Trail Creek or Bald Mountain.

in town from the inn, and Ketchum's many fine shops entice shoppers and people browsing for year-round sports clothing. The town also supports art galleries and a wide variety of restaurants.

For indoor recreation, and of special interest to business travelers, guests of the inn may enjoy the million-dollar athletic club only a half-block away. The facility is fully equipped with a lap pool, weights and aerobic equipment, and is available to guests at a special discounted rate.

Getting There

Fly into Hailey Airport, south of Ketchum and head north on U.S. 75, turn left at Rivers Street, just beyond the Trail Creek Bridge. The inn is two blocks toward the mountains, on your left. There is plenty of parking in front of the inn.

IDAHO ROCKY MOUNTAIN RANCH

Address: HC 64, Box 9934, Stanley, Idaho 83278
Telephone: (208) 774-3544
Location: On Scenic Highway 75, 50 miles north of the Sun
                   Valley/Ketchum area and 10 miles south of Stanley
Hosts: Bill and Jeana Leavell, Managers
Room Rates: Summer rooms and cabins: $48/night, per person
                   double occupancy, $290/week, includes full break-
                   fast. Dinners $13 to $20. Winter bed & breakfast
                   cabins: $85 to $125, $15 per additional guest,
                   includes full breakfast.
Credit Cards: MasterCard, Visa
Remarks: Dinner served 6:30 p.m. and 8:30 p.m.; reserva-
                   tions required. Dining room open to the public.
                   Horses are welcome; reservations recommended.
                   No other pets. No snowmobiles. No smoking
                   except on the porches.

Bordered by the White Cloud Mountains to the east and the Sawtooth Mountains to the west, the Sawtooth Valley is one of Idaho's precious treasures. Winding through the scenic valley are the headwaters of the legendary Salmon River, where remnants of once abundant salmon and steelhead trout populations travel 900 miles from the Pacific Ocean to spawn. It is here, in the heart of the Sawtooth National Recreation Area in central Idaho, where you'll find the Idaho Rocky Mountain Ranch.

Originally part of an old homestead, the 1,000 acres that became the Idaho Rocky Mountain Club were acquired by Winston Paul, a Frigidaire distributor from New York who constructed the impressive lodgepole pine lodge and cabins in 1930 to entertain his guests. We hear that most of what you see today is as it was over 60 years ago, right down to the monogrammed china. In 1951 the ranch was purchased by Ed and Ruth Bogert. Today, under the guidance of their daughter, the Idaho Rocky Mountain Ranch offers to the public warm Idaho hospitality and an atmosphere that lets you forget the rat race you left behind.

Log Cabin Living

The ranch features nine authentic log duplex cabins handsomely decorated with handmade log and willow furniture, and rock fireplaces. Each cabin sleeps two with a choice of queen or twin beds. All have private bathrooms and most have handcrafted oakley stone showers, the twin bed cabins also offer tubs, complete with bubble bath. For larger parties, cabins are available with connecting doors.

The main lodge is home to four cozy guest rooms with private baths with showers. These offer a choice of double or twin beds. In the name of serenity, neither the cabins or the lodge rooms come equipped with private phones or televisions.

In the front lobby of the lodge, you'll find comfortable cushion chairs around a fireplace for socializing. Bookshelves well stocked with area brochures, while a hostess bar offers beer, wine, non-alcoholic beverages and other goodies for sale. The ranch also makes a perfect spot for weddings, receptions, private parties or business meetings and retreats for 10 to 150 people.

Dining by the Fire

Ranch guests wake up to crisp mountain mornings with a buffet of freshly brewed coffee, fruit juices, baked goods, cereal and fresh fruit for starters. For those with bigger appetites, the ranch serves a hot breakfast from 7:30 a.m. to 10 a.m. featuring specialties such as "eggs quesadillas," scrambled eggs with onion, ham, peppers and cheese wrapped in a tortilla and served with ranch salsa, or an endless stack of sourdough blueberry pancakes dripping with butter and hot maple syrup.

Dinnertime offers outstanding entrees and the soothing sounds of an acoustic guitar. The huge rock fireplace is the dining room's focal point and lends to the romantic ranch atmosphere. Directly out the windows are the Sawtooth Mountains. One of our favorite dinner entrees is the Idaho ruby rainbow trout stuffed with artichoke hearts, sliced mushrooms, green onions and dill. Save room for dessert for the ranch always offers four to five home-baked selections.

Endless Outdoor Activities

The ranch makes an ideal home base from which to explore the outdoor activities literally at your finger tips. White-water rafting experiences are close. The ranch has a horse riding program and endless trails. In fact, the ranch would be happy to house your horse from home. If you're a hiker, venture out on the trails leading right from the ranch. Mountain biking (bikes are available for rent in Stanley) and mountaineering are also popular pastimes in the area.

Better yet, simply stay put on the ranch where there's plenty of quiet time and an unsurpassed view of the Sawtooths directly from the porch of the main lodge. "Many people love to sit on the porch playing checkers or chess and watch a Sawtooth day go by," says Co-manager Jeana Leavell. Sooth those weary bones in the ranch's natural hot spring pool on the bank of the Salmon River.

Come winter, when several feet of snow blanket the basin, and deer and elk winter in the valley, the ranch transforms into a quaint bed &

The fire-warmed dining room faces the Sawtooth Mountains.

breakfast and a haven for cross-country skiers. Ski enthusiasts can tour on the ranch and in surrounding Forest Service lands. With advance notice, the ranch can arrange for guided backcountry ski tours, ski instruction, even catered picnic lunches or dinners.

Winter accommodations are located at the lower ranch, next to the hot springs swimming pool and consist of comfortable one- and three-bedroom cabins with kitchens, private bathrooms, wood stoves and back-up electric heat. The cabins come fully stock with towels, linens, dishes and cooking ware, coffee makers, ovens, refrigerators and small stereos. Due to the abundant wildlife that winters near the ranch, pets and snowmobiles are not allowed.

Getting There

From the Sun Valley/Ketchum area, travel 50 miles north on Highway 75 over Galena Summit and into the Sawtooth Valley. Turn right at the Idaho Rocky Mountain Ranch sign. The ranch sits against the tree line about half a mile from the highway. From Stanley, travel about 10 miles south on Highway 75 and take a left at the sign.

KANDAHAR LODGE

Address: Big Mountain Ski Resort Village, P.O. Box 1659, Whitefish, MT 59937

Telephone: (406) 862-6098; toll free (800) 858-5439; FAX (406) 862-6095

Location: On Big Mountain, eight miles north of Whitefish

Hosts: Buck and Mary Pat Love

Room Rates: $76 single, $82 double, $140 suites (summer); $84 to $134 rooms, $116 to $156 lofts, $194 two-room suites (winter). Weekly rates, season packages and one-bedroom apartments are also available.

Credit Cards: American Express, MasterCard, Visa

Remarks: Children under 12 stay free.

Kandahar is an obscure town in Afghanistan that was, in August 1880, the location of a besieged British garrison. British General Frederick Roberts and his troops marched to it's rescue. The brave act earned him knighthood and the name Lord Roberts of Kandahar. Years later, he sponsored the Roberts of Kandahar Challenge Cup, and was involved in the creation of the Kandahar Ski Club, which sponsored the first international ski meet in which the winner is chosen on the basis of combined downhill and slalom race scores.

And so it came to pass that Buck and Mary Pat Love, two ski devotees with an admiration for the grand style of European ski lodges, chose to name their 50- room alpine ski lodge in Whitefish, Montana, "Kandahar."

European Style Lodge

Mary Pat and Buck wanted to create an entire package - great skiing, beautiful scenery, and first class lodging and dining. As Mary Pat explains, "From the start we decided our first priority was to spend as much time as possible with our guests; we are both committed to making them feel comfortable, relaxed and at home." To put their philosophy to work, they built their home as part of the lodge and live there with their two daughters, Lindsay and Hailey. They are, in the best sense of the word, innkeepers.

Their "inn" is a warm and wonderful three-story European style lodge built around a central sunken lobby with an immense rock fireplace, an array of comfortable sofas and chairs flanked by reading lamps, period antiques, and original landscape art. The walls are sided with knotty cedar and massive support beams carry the ceil-

ing. The entrance to the lodge has window arches and side panels of etched glass that display mountain and forest scenes by local Whitefish artist Myni Ferguson. On either side of the lobby, wide carpeted staircases lead guests to their second- and third-floor rooms, suites or lofts. You can choose from rooms designed for one to eight people. Sixteen of the 48 units have small fully stocked kitchens. The rooms have cedar paneling, sand colored carpets, pine furniture and down comforters on the beds. Our favorite room has a large front room, with queen-sized sofa bed, television, telephone, kitchen, dining table and bath. The attached bedroom has a king-sized bed, bathroom, comfortable chairs, dressers and television.

Cafe Kandahar

Nestled into the flank of the lodge is the compact Cafe Kandahar. In the morning, guests can take their breakfast at the sturdy wooden tables. It's in the evening when the Cafe takes on a special warm glow. Your host might suggest your meal start with "Oysters Kandahar", served cajun style. In addition to the two nightly specials, you can always count on entrees such as the marinated chicken breasts, done with Montana hothouse tomatoes and artichokes; or fresh sea Scallop fettuccini with a garlic-basil pesto. The cafe does not sell liquor, however, guests can bring in their own bottle for consumption during dinner.

Year-Round Enjoyment

Kandahar Lodge is open year-round and offers guests an assortment of activities. In the summer season (May to October), guests can make the cool mountain resort their home base and take day trips to majestic Glacier National Park, hike in the rugged Mission Mountains, sail on the astonishingly blue Flathead Lake, and shop in the nearby towns of Whitefish and Kalispell. For the outdoor enthusiast, there is boating, waterskiing and fishing on Whitefish Lake, and several million acres of designated wilderness to explore. The lodge has golf packages at seven nearby courses. The mountain operates the gondola lift to the top of Big Mountain, a must do activity while you're there. Eagle watchers flock to West Glacier to catch sight of the showy birds in October.

Buck and Mary Pat are avid sailors as well as skiers. Each April, you will find them participating in the North American Ski/Yachting Championships, which take place on Big Mountain and Flathead Lake. For sailors who ski and skiers who sail, this event provides the perfect combination of mountain skiing and sailing on the nearly frozen waters of Flathead.

In the winter months (November to April), snow comes early and stays late. Big Mountain and the Kandahar Lodge are often blessed

Wide carpeted stairs lead to second and third-floor guest rooms.

with fresh, powdery snow. *Ski Magazine* called 7,000-foot Big Mountain "one of the best ski areas in the world." The mountain receives over 300 inches of snowfall; you can ski 3,000 acres on 50 marked trails using eight lifts, including a high speed quad and gondola. This claim is hard to dispute. Daytime tickets cost $15 to $29; night skiing tickets are $9. Children six and under ski free. Cross-country skiers have miles of trails and roads to glide over, too.

There is a ski trail from the mountain to the lodge, making the return trip easy. Once there, skiers can enter the warm boot room, lock up their gear and walk in stocking feet directly to one of the two saunas or to the jacuzzi for a relaxing slow soak in the 102-degree water.

Getting There

From Whitefish, turn right onto Wisconsin Avenue (Highway 487) and follow the signs to Big Mountain. Kandahar Lodge is about eight miles north of Whitefish. Amtrak serves Whitefish. Buses and taxis ferry passengers to the mountaintop. Delta and Horizon airlines have daily flights to Kalispell, 45 minutes from the Lodge.

FLATHEAD LAKE LODGE

Address: P.O. Box 248, Bigfork, MT 59911
Telephone: (406) 837-4391; FAX (406) 837-6977
Location: Highway 35, one mile south of Bigfork
Hosts: Doug and Maureen Averill
Weekly Rates: Adults $1,295, teenagers $987, children from 4 -
                    12 $797, children under 4 $96, single occupancy
                    $1,426. Rates Sunday to Sunday.
Credit Cards: American Express, MasterCard, Visa, and personal
                    checks
Remarks: No pets. Open May through September.
                    Reservations required.

Since 1945, the Averill family's Flathead Lake Lodge and Dude Ranch has been offering their guests a full week of lodging, meals and recreational activities on their 2,000-acre ranch on the east shore of Flathead Lake. The lodge caters to families with children of all ages, and the 100 guests are limited only by their inability to do everything at once. *Sunset, Better Homes and Gardens and Travel and Leisure* have all featured the lodge for its ability to provide one of the finest family vacations in America.

The Wranglers

"People come here for the horses," says Doug Averill, an ex-rodeo rider and manager of the ranch. "We have dude horses for the inexperienced riders and quality quarterhorses for those who know how to handle that kind of horse. A lot of our guests are simply nuts about horses." So the Averills give them horses—morning, noon and night. Guests can sign up for breakfast rides, group rides, family rides or fast rides. The wranglers start their day at 5:30 a.m., but even at that hour there are kids down at the stable to help them brush and feed the horses.

At the end of the week there is a kid's rodeo. They participate in barrel races, pole bending contests, three-legged races and the water balloon challenge. "The rodeo is for fun. It's not meant to be competitive," Doug explains. Once a week, a roping club comes to the ranch to put on a performance, and Buck, a longtime ranch hand, entertains guests with stories and demonstrations of old-time skills such as braiding rope.

As much as guests love the horses, it would be impossible to forget the lake. The clear blue waters of Flathead lap at the shore of the ranch, and guests are encouraged to take out the sailboats, fishing boats, canoes and windsurfers at their leisure. There's waterskiing

everyday at 1 p.m., and an experienced waterfront hand (referred to as a water wimp by the wranglers) is nearby to handle the powerboat and give lessons.

Guests can now enjoy a thrilling sail aboard two historic Q Class racing sloops. These are 51 foot long oak and mahogany classics, designed by L. Francis Herreshoff during the roaring 20s era. Each of the boats has a famous racing history. I don't know of any other place to offer such an interesting adventure to their guests.

For those who prefer the flowing water of a river, the lodge offers raft trips and inner tube floats on the Swan and Flathead rivers or take a raft fishing trip with the lodge's flyfishing guide.

If the horses and the lake don't take up all of your free time, you can play tennis, volleyball or basketball, swim in the lake or pool, attend the nightly beach fires and sing-alongs, work in the ranch's vegetable and flower garden, take a day trip to Glacier National Park, or just sit on one of the dozens of benches, chairs or lounges that are spread around the ranch. A game room monitor takes kids on nature hikes to gather the raw materials for future projects- painted rock people and pinecone cowboys. There are, in fact, only two things that guests can't do on the ranch, they can't watch television and they can't play video games.

The Lodge

The Civilian Conservation Corps built the Main Lodge and the South Lodge in 1932, and both two-story Western structures have large lobbies with huge river rock fireplaces. The Main Lodge houses the office, Saddle Sore Saloon (guests bring their own liquor), kitchen and family style dining room and a few rooms for single guests. The walls of the lobby are decorated with trophies of past hunting expeditions. The 25 to 30 families that arrive at the ranch each Sunday are housed in 17 cottages and cabins, which accommodate four to six people. Each unit has its own bath, two or three bedrooms, a comfortable living room and Western furnishings.

Family Style Dining

The lodge and dude ranch are completely self-sustaining. The kitchen staff bakes the bread, plans the desserts and prepares all the meals. Breakfast might consist of huckleberry pancakes and bacon and eggs one day and omelettes the next. Coffee is always served first thing in the morning, so you can have that first cup while standing next to a crackling fire in the Main Lodge. Lunch is light: salads and quiche or food that the kids like—hamburgers and soups. If the weather cooperates, and it usually does in the summer, lunch is served outside on the deck overlooking the lake.

The lodge buildings face Flathead Lake.

Dinner might be a steak fry, fresh salmon, chicken, prime rib or a whole pig.

The unique combination of the lodge, its setting and recreational activities give the Averills an almost unheard-of repeat rate. Over 60 percent of Flathead Lake Lodge's guests come back. Mr. George Wood holds the record, he has come every summer for the last 42 years, never missing the first two weeks of August. George became known as Grandpa George and even gave Maureen Averill, Doug's wife, away on her wedding day.

Getting There

From Polson, follow Highway 35 north along the east side of Flathead Lake. The sign for the ranch is about one mile south of Bigfork. From Glacier National Park, take Highway 2 toward Columbia Falls, turn onto 206, heading south. It will join with Highway 35, which will lead you past Bigfork and one mile south to the ranch.

LONE MOUNTAIN RANCH

Address: P.O. Box 160069, Big Sky, MT. 59716
Telephone: (406) 995-4644; FAX (406) 995-4670
Location: Four and one-half miles off Highway 191
Hosts: Bob and Vivian Schaap
Rates: $988 per person per week, double. Includes three meals a day, airport transportation and a wide variety of recreational activities. Reduced rates for families with small children.
Credit Cards: Discover, MasterCard, Visa
Remarks: Open June through October; December through April. Reservations required. No pets.

Nestled in its own secluded valley next to a clear mountain stream, Lone Mountain Ranch is a dream destination for lovers of the outdoors. Summer family fun, spectacular fly-fishing, horseback riding, children's program, naturalist guided interpretative hikes and Yellowstone tours, and winter cross-country skiing adventures are all packaged to include comfortable Western lodging and ranch meals in a friendly, informal atmosphere. With its close proximity (20 miles) to the natural wonders of Yellowstone National Park, Lone Mountain Ranch provides guests with enough activities to keep them actively happy for way longer than a week's visit allows.

Prettiest Spot On Earth

The original ranch buildings were built in 1926 using hand-hewed logs. Originally a working cattle operation, Bob and Vivian Schaap took over the ranch in 1977 to create a cross-country ski center and summer guest ranch. The 23 immaculate cabins accommodate guests, with all the comforts of home- cozy fireplaces, electric heat, private baths and even front porches. The cabins are furnished with lodgepole pine furniture and each possesses its own character. Many guests reserve the same special cabin year after year. With the ranch's excellent airline access, great snow and magnificent surroundings, it's not hard to understand why the Schaaps think they are "lucky to live in just about the prettiest spot on Earth."

Ranch Cooking With Gourmet Flair

An active day at the ranch will certainly build hearty appetites. The dinner bell is always a welcome sound. Guests are treated to nationally acclaimed ranch cuisine. Three abundant meals are presented daily in the relaxed, smoke-free, atmosphere of the ranch's beautiful

new log dining lodge. Delicious sack lunches are prepared for guests who choose to be out and about at lunchtime. In the summer, there are special weekly dinners scheduled - a dinner horse ride, steak barbecue, a campfire sing-along and a morning breakfast cookout. Special diet requests are easily accommodated.

Summer Family Fun

The ranch successfully integrates activities for guests of all ages. Children can choose from a variety of interesting adventures including campouts in an authentic teepee, horseback rides, rodeos, nature walks and orienteering. Little ones are supervised at the Lodgepole playground, and babysitting is available a few afternoons a week.

Horseback trips are a favorite activity for adults, too. Sunday is reserved for matching guests with horses. Monday through Saturday you can saddle up for a half-day ride to the Spanish Peaks or an all-day trip into Yellowstone National Park. Ranch wranglers accompany the small groups and are quick to point out the backcountry wildlife, flowers and natural features.

Guests can shake out their saddle sores by swing dancing to lively Western music, enjoying a massage or soaking in the hot tub under the big Montana sky. Evening entertainment may also include ballads of mountain men lore and grizzly bear tales accompanied by a Western guitar. The beautiful new ranch saloon is a comfortable and smoke-free spot to share recent adventure stories.

We particularly like the ranch's popular naturalist program. Yellowstone interpretive trips offer guests opportunities to explore the park's famous features as well as its better-kept secrets. Naturalist-guided nature walks are offered several times a week. We find the best time to go is during the fall. The lack of crowds draw the Yellowstone animals down from the high country, making them easier to see.

Lone Mountain Ranch is one of the few places in the West to have it's fly-fishing program included in the Orvis-endorsed list. Fishing adventures can include wading, float-tubing or fishing from a drift boat. Fall is our favorite time to fish the nearby world famous, blue-ribbon trout streams.

Cross Country Skier's Paradise

Located right in the middle of deep powder snow country, the ranch is an ideal destination for a nordic holiday. The ranch has 45 miles of professionally groomed trails that begin right outside the cabin doors. First-track telemarking enthusiasts can anticipate miles of backcountry blanketed by virgin snow. The ranch has a full-service

Guests enjoy nationally acclaimed ranch cuisine in the smoke free dining room.

ski shop, complete with rental and demo equipment. Professional instructors teach beginning fundamentals and skills for more advanced skiers. All-day guided trips to Yellowstone and the Spanish Peaks are available throughout the week. We have found few things that compare to the thrill of skiing through geyser basins, past snow-ghosted trees, frozen waterfalls, and wintering herds of elk and bison.

A highlight of the week, and a must on the "to do" list, is the evening horse-drawn sleigh ride up to the North Fork Cabin for a prime rib dinner, cooked on a 100 year old wood cook stove. The meal is accompanied by delightful musical entertainment.

Getting There

From the north, exit off Interstate 90 at Bozeman. Go south on Highway 191 through the Gallatin Canyon for 40 miles. Turn right at the Big Sky Resort turnoff. Proceed up the Big Sky Spur Road 4.5 miles to the Lone Mountain Ranch sign. From Yellowstone, exit the west entrance of the park and drive 48 miles north on Highway 191 to the Big Sky Resort turnoff. Turn left and proceed as above.

MOUNTAIN SKY GUEST RANCH

Address: Big Creek Road, Emigrant, MT (P.O. Box 1128
                  Bozeman, MT 59771 for reservations)
Telephone: (406) 587-1244; toll free (800) 548-3392
Location: Four and one-half miles up Big Creek Road, off
                  Highway 89 in south central Montana
Hosts: Shirley Arsenault, Manager; Alan and Mary
                  Brutger, Proprietors
Room Rates: Individual rates per week —Adults $1,330 to
                  $1,505, Children 7-12 $1,155 to $1,295, six and
                  under $875 to $1015
Credit Cards: MasterCard, Visa
Remarks: Open June to October. Reservations required.

One of the most remarkable things about Mountain Sky Guest Ranch is the number of familiar faces we see each time we visit. From the seasonal kids' counselors and ranch-hands to the growing and changing faces of the children who return each year with their families, people just can't seem to get enough of this place.

Mountain Sky was built in the 1930s, the old cabins, the lodge and their furniture were crafted with wood taken right off the property. The original cabins and split-log furniture are still in use, but are blended today with new furnishings to provide a warm, relaxed setting for a family vacation.

Cabins: Rustic and Contemporary

The main lodge has three massive rock fireplaces, braided rugs over wooden floors and a piano made from rough-hewn lodgepole pine. The main lodge houses a comfortable great room, the kitchen, the lounge and bar, two dining rooms, a meeting room and the office.

The original log cabins have been remodeled to include all the modern conveniences and comfort. These one-, two- and three-bedroom cabins have a rock fireplace or wood burning stove and Western hand-hewn furniture. Newer cabins feature spacious sitting rooms, wall-to-wall carpeting and comfortable furniture. There are also small refrigerators, coffee makers, private baths and generous closets. These cabins sleep two to six. There are several three-bedroom cabins available. All of the cabins at Mountain Sky have daily housekeeping, an inviting front porch with hanging flower baskets and a basket of fresh fruit replenished daily. Guests may use telephones in the lodge, but don't look for telephones or televisions in the cabins, because there aren't any.

The week at Mountain Sky begins on Sunday. Guests can use the afternoon to freshen up, unpack, walk down to the stable or tennis courts, or enjoy a complimentary drink poolside while getting to know their neighbors.

For horse lovers there are breakfast, morning and afternoon rides over miles of trails on the ranch and adjacent Gallatin National Forest. Riders can spot deer, elk and moose amid the rock cliffs, grassy meadows and forested slopes of the ranch. The week's riding activities culminate with a "showdeo" in which children are encouraged to show off their skills in events such as pole bending and egg-on-spoon races.

Fly-fishing is a major attraction at the ranch. There is a trained instructor on staff to teach the basics. You can practice your casting at the private trout pond or try your luck in Big Creek, on the ranch. For more world-class trout fishing, visit the nearby Yellowstone River, Nelson and Armstrong spring creeks or any of the fabled rivers in near-by Yellowstone Park.The ranch sponsors fly-fishing clinics during the fall. Those attending get all the Mountain Sky amenities plus guest speakers, demonstrations and lessons.

Whether your favorite vacation pursuit is hiking, playing tennis on championship courts or just relaxing in the hot tub, heated pool or sauna, Mountain Sky provides the arena. Volleyball, billiards, ping-pong and horseshoes are also favored pastimes on the ranch.

Evenings are capped off by a variety of entertainment. A typical week may include Western dance instruction, a folk concert, dancing to a local combo and sing-a-longs at the piano led by staff or guests. Often the kids will host an evening of great entertainment and skits, much to the delight of all the guests.

Vacation For All

Although this is a family-oriented ranch, Alan, Mary and their friendly staff know very well that parents need a vacation, too. Experienced counselors supervise nature walks, swimming, games and fishing. A children's wrangler gives guidance and instruction on horsemanship and special "Kids' Dinners" are prepared, followed by activities such as a hayride, Indian pow wow or softball. This allows the adults to fully enjoy the gourmet cuisine. Mountain Sky Ranch has the best developed childrens program we have ever experienced.

Mountain air and activity work up mighty appetites. Long before you arise, the staff is busy setting up the buffet tables, ladened with pastries, cinnamon rolls, croissants and muffins, all freshly baked each morning. Soon after you hear the ring of the Wrangler's Bell, you can choose from made-to-order omelettes, ham and eggs, fresh fruit, granola or blueberry pancakes. The Lunchtime offers a casual buffet, served outside, with a choice of ethnic speciality foods, such

The beautiful ranch is 30 miles north of Yellowstone Park.

as Tex-Mex, Italian pasta selections or Cajun fish. Dinners at Mountain Sky are exceptional. Fresh seafood is flown in from the coast, the best of Montana produce and beef are served. Hors d' oeuvres are served in the warmth of the Mountain View Lounge before dinner. The dinner may be a continental fare, a fresh salmon or mesquite grilled rack of lamb. The ranch has an extensive wine collection to complement any selection.

A visit to 3,000 square-mile Yellowstone Park, 30 miles away, is about the only reason to leave Mountain Sky Guest Ranch. The natural phenomena are the primary attractions here; the geysers, canyons, prairie, hot springs, lakes and wildlife are not to be missed.

Getting There

Turn off Interstate 90 at Livingston and head south on Highway 89 for 30 miles. Look for the sign for Mountain Sky Guest Ranch at the Big Creek Road turn-off. Be advised that the 4.5 miles to the ranch are slow. For travelers headed to the ranch from Yellowstone, the Mountain Sky turn-off will be on the left-hand side of Highway 89, 30 miles north of Gardiner.

BROOKS LAKE LODGE

Address: P.O. Box 594, Dubois, WY 82513
Telephone: (307) 455-2121; FAX (307) 455-2121
Location: 60 miles east of Jackson; 28 miles west of Dubois,
Hosts: Will and Rebecca Rigsby, General Managers;
                        Richard and Barbara Carlsberg, Proprietors
Room Rates: Winter rates (Dec. 15 - April 15): lodge rooms
                        $115; cabin suites $140; includes dinner and
                        breakfast. Summer rates (July 1 - Sept. 15): lodge
                        rooms $150; cabin suites $170; includes all meals,
                        horseback riding and canoeing; Three night mini-
                        mum.
Credit Cards: American Express, MasterCard, Visa
Remarks: No smoking inside lodge except in front lobby and
                        bar. No pets. Lodge rooms are handicapped acces-
                        sible.

Tucked away in a pristine valley at the base of the Continental Divide in northwestern Wyoming is a lodge steeped in history and folklore. The Brooks Lake Lodge offers the ultimate in wilderness adventure and backwoods tranquility. Originally constructed in 1922 to house overnight bus travelers in route to Yellowstone National Park, the lodge was converted to a dude ranch, the Diamond G Ranch. After changing hands several times, the lodge found a friend when Richard Carlsberg and his wife, Barbara, purchased the lodge in 1987. They began the restoration of the lodge. In December 1988, the Brooks Lake Lodge reopened in all its glory. The Carlsberg's daughter, Rebecca, and her husband, Will Rigsby, manage the lodge.

Rusticity and Romance

The massive log lodge is listed in the National Register of Historic Places. Nearly all of the furniture in the lodge is antique or hand-crafted works of Wyoming artists. Furnished in wicker and dripping with rusticity and romance, the Great Hall houses an impressive collection of wild game mounts from 'round the world. The Carlsbergs tell us that some of the same craftsmen that worked on the Brooks Lake Lodge are ones who had toiled on the legendary Old Faithful Lodge in Yellowstone. Its size and atmosphere make the Great Hall an ideal place for holding large parties, dances, weddings or corporate meetings.

The lodge features six guest rooms tastefully decorated in lodgepole pine furnishings and named after the area's indigenous wildlife — grizzly, elk, bison, deer, moose and antelope. Behind the lodge, nes-

tled in the trees, are six cabins that offer a little more privacy. Each cabin is equipped with a wood-burning stove (in addition to electric heat) and private bath, many with clawfooted tubs. The cabins are distinct in character, each decorated according to its name. The Prospector's Cabin features picks, lanterns and other gold-mining paraphernalia. An authentic judge's robe hangs in the Judge's Cabin while the walls of the Fisherman's Cabin are hung with creels, rods and other fishing gear. You won't find any telephones or televisions in the rooms (a phone is available for guest use in the bar). You will find bathrobes in each room, which come in handy for trips back and forth to the large indoor jacuzzi.

Hearty, Western Fare

A day at the lodge begins with a generous buffet of fresh fruit, cold cereal, breads and muffins, followed by an entree that may include piping hot eggs, bacon, pancakes or French toast. For lunch you can count on homemade soups, thick, hearty chili during cold winter days, pasta salads, and main dishes such as chicken breasts or flank steak. If your plans call for spending the day hiking into the back-country, the lodge will pack you a sack lunch. During the winter, the lodge serves lunch to the public as well.

At 4 p.m., join others for afternoon tea in the front lobby. Cookies, English finger sandwiches and other baked goods will hold you over until dinner. Dining at the lodge is every bit a Western tradition — steaks served with baked potatoes and broccoli with peach cobbler for dessert, or Cornish game hens or grilled swordfish served with rice and vegetables with Rebecca's favorite, chocolate mousse.

Before or after dinner, mosey into the Diamond G Saloon for drinks, a game of pool, darts or quiet conversation. The saloon, which offers a full bar, opens at 6 p.m. for hors d'oeuvres and during the winter also from 11 a.m. to 3 p.m. for fun and games. The only television in the lodge is found here and reserved for children's videos and the showing of "Jubal," a 1956 Western starring Glenn Ford and Ernest Borgnine filmed in, you got it, the Diamond G Saloon.

An Outdoor Lover's Paradise

Brooks Lake Lodge is a winter paradise for snowmobilers and cross-country skiers. Bring your own equipment or rent snowmobiles from the lodge; use of cross-country skis is included in your room rate. Other popular activities include snowshoeing, ice fishing and, believe it or not, dancing and singing on frozen Brooks Lake. Downhill skiing is only 60 miles away in Jackson. Yellowstone and Grant Teton national parks offer countless other possibilities.

Afternoon tea is served in the Main Lodge each day at 4:00 p.m.

Summer brings a whole new look to Brooks Lake Lodge — lush green meadows, colorful wildflowers and crystal clear lakes. Surrounded by the Shoshone National Forest, the lodge offers miles and miles of hiking and horse trails. The lodge has a string of trail horses and all guests are provided with their own horse for the duration of their stay. Hike or ride up to one of the many lakes, where the Carlsbergs have likely stashed a canoe or two for your pleasure. If you're a fisherman at heart, nearby lakes and streams offer premier fishing for cutthroat, brook and rainbow trout. The lodge provides fishing guides and tackle to guests.

Getting There

From Jackson, take Highway 26/87 north to Moran. From Moran, take Highway 26/287 southeast to Brooks Lake Road and turn left. The lodge is five miles up the road. From the east, take Highway 26/287 to Brooks Lake Road and turn right.

RUSTY PARROT LODGE

Address: P.O. Box 1657, 175 N. Jackson, Jackson, WY
                  83001
Telephone: (307) 733-2000, toll free (800) 458-2004;
                  FAX (307) 733-5566
Location: Three blocks from the town square
Hosts: Ron and Gayla Harrison, Owners
Room Rates: $125 to $185 double
Credit Cards: American Express, Carte Blanche, Diners Club,
                  Discover, MasterCard, Visa
Remarks: Rates include full Jackson breakfast, HBO and local
                  phone calls. No smoking in the inn. No pets.

Ron and Gayla Harrison had been on the lookout for a small inn to purchase for 15 years when they decided that if they couldn't find the perfect place, they would just have to build it. In 1990, the Rusty Parrot opened in Jackson Hole, Wyoming. A combination of everything the Harrisons had loved in other resorts and their original ideas, the Rusty Parrot reflects the early Western heritage of Jackson Hole, while retaining modern comfort and convenience.

A major component of this convenience is the inn staff. "Everybody here is devoted to making sure our guests have a good time. We try to create an atmosphere that's like a visit with close friends," Ron says. "every once in awhile I come down at night and find a guest sound asleep by the fire." Gayla and Ron live in the lodge and are on hand to attend to your comfort or to join you for a cup of tea. Their daughter, Heidi, an internationally trained and certified massage therapist, provides this service to the guests of the lodge.

Western Tradition

The Rusty Parrot is furnished in a tradition created in the pioneer days. "People traveling west often would bring one piece of furniture that was very special to them, or perhaps a piece of cloth. Everything else would be handmade once they arrived," explains Ron. In front of the large stone fireplace in the gathering room is a large table hand-hewn by Ron, and his antler chandelier lights the dining room. Limited edition prints and photographs from famous wildlife photographers hang in guest rooms.

Throughout the lodge, Gayla's sharp eye for interior design is in evidence, from the wreaths on the wall to wildflower arrangements that brighten the rooms. At Christmas, she makes ornaments for the tree, which Ron and their guests bring in from the forest. The Gathering Room is the place for breakfast, afternoon tea with cookies and hot

chocolate, and of course, gathering. A rocking chair is perfect for reading by the fire, and tables scattered across the room provide places to play games or to enjoy a snack.

The 31 guest rooms also mirror pioneering values. The beds are made with handcrafted lodgepole pine and near-by are twisted oak tables, and chairs with rawhide seats and backs. All rooms have one or two queen-sized beds, wool trade blankets and goosedown comforters. For a slightly more modern touch, armoires conceal the room's 26" television. Also on the beds, you'll find one of the Harrison's teddy bears. "We don't want anybody to be lonely in Jackson," Ron says. You'll definitely stay warm in your room; all are furnished with big terry robes and have oversized oval tubs in their private baths. Nearly half of the rooms have fireplaces, three of which also have jacuzzi tubs for two set before the fire.

Jackson Breakfast

"Breakfast is a serious affair," Ron notes, before listing the range of breakfast items. "You can have as much as you want to eat." Served from 7 a.m. to 10 a.m., you can eat in the gathering room with other guests or enjoy your meal in the privacy of your room. There is no set menu at the Rusty Parrot; the chefs make something new every day. Banana Belgian waffles with honey-sizzled apricot sauce, trout almondine and pancakes with cranberry, raspberry and orange syrup are a few of their recent creations.

Out and About

You'll need every bit of that breakfast, too, if you are to take full advantage of the activities available in and around Jackson Hole. The lodge is close to three major Wyoming ski resorts, making it an ideal spot for a winter sojourn. Jackson Hole Ski Area has the greatest vertical drop of any ski area in the United States, and also features fine intermediate and beginner slopes. A shuttle to Grand Targhee Ski Resort stops at the lodge each morning, taking skiers to what Gayla calls "the best powder in the United States." You can watch the night skiing at Snow King from the steaming outdoor hot tub on the Rusty Parrot's upper deck.

Other winter activities include snowmobile rides to Yellowstone National Park , dogsled tours of the Jackson area and cross-country skiing. You can also take a sleigh ride through the evening wilderness. The Harrisons also coordinate a series of topical discussions, such as biopolitics or Wyoming poets, with the Snake River Institute. Ask them for details on "Wyoming Explored."

Throughout the year, you can see more wildlife here than perhaps anywhere else in the country. Animal safaris are led by the Great Plains Wildlife Institute; elk, bison, moose, bighorn sheep, eagles

The Gathering Room is the spot for breakfast and social activities.

and coyote are just a few of the animals you'll see through the spotting scopes mounted on the jeep top. Summer is the busiest time in Jackson Hole. You can go whitewater and scenic rafting, fly-fishing, horseback riding, mountain biking and rock climbing. In town, visit the Cowboy Bar, with saddles for barstools and two-step lessons every Thursday. Jackson Hole is also the Western art capital, and you can travel the wooden boardwalks from gallery to gallery. Wednesdays and Saturdays are rodeo nights. Our favorite time to visit is during the fall, with the vibrant colors of the trees, the crisp, comfortable weather and the more relaxed atmosphere.

Getting There

Entering Jackson from the north (Yellowstone and Grand Teton National Parks) turn right at the second stop light on Gill Ave. and go three blocks west. From the south, watch for the large bronze elk sculpture in front of the Wyoming Wildlife Museum. Turn left at the next corner, which is Jackson.The lodge is two blocks north at the corner of Jackson and Gill, opposite Miller Park. Jackson is served by American, Continental, Delta, United and Skywest Airlines.

SPECIAL INDEXES

Column headers (left to right):
Restaurant open to the public · No. of people for meeting facilities · Kitchens available in some rooms · Fireplaces in some rooms · Facilities for the handicapped · Spas or hot tubs available · Swimming pool on premises · Tennis on premises · Golf available · Horses available · Boating available · Fishing on premises · Children under 12 welcome · Spectacular views · Pets welcome

California

	Restaurant	Meeting #	Kitchens	Fireplaces	Handicapped	Spas/hot tubs	Swimming pool	Tennis	Golf	Horses	Boating	Fishing	Children <12	Spectacular views	Pets
Casa Tropicana	●	80	●	●	●	●								●	
Blue Lantern Inn		25	●	●		●			●		●		●	●	
Villa Rosa		18	●	●		●	●								
Simpson House		25	●	●		●			●	●	●			●	
The Alisal Ranch		150	●			●	●	●	●	●	●	●	●	●	●
Ballard Inn		30	●	●					●	●				●	
Garden Street Inn		13	●	●		●			●						
Martine Inn		24	●	●		●								●	
Inn Depot Hill		8	●	●		●			●		●				
Babbling Brook Inn		12	●						●		●				
Inn at Union Square		60	●	●		●								●	
Washington Square Inn				●										●	
Mansion at Lakewood		60	●			●	●								
Wine And Roses Country Inn	●	12													
Amber House		25				●			●	●					
Beazley House															
Wine Country Inn				●		●	●							●	
Silver Rose Inn		10				●	●							●	
Belle De Jour				●		●									
Whale Watch Inn			●	●		●						●		●	
Stanford Inn		20	●	●	●	●	●				●	●	●	●	●
Gingerbread Mansion				●											
Carter House	●	10		●		●								●	

Pacific Northwest

	Restaurant	Meeting #	Kitchens	Fireplaces	Handicapped	Spas/hot tubs	Swimming pool	Tennis	Golf	Horses	Boating	Fishing	Children <12	Spectacular views	Pets
Romeo Inn		20	●	●		●	●							●	
Paradise Ranch	●	50	●			●			●	●	●	●	●	●	
Rock Springs Ranch		50	●	●		●			●	●		●	●	●	
Black Butte Ranch	●	35	●	●		●	●	●	●	●			●	●	●
The Heathman Hotel	●	150				●								●	
Columbia Gorge Hotel	●	200	●	●									●	●	●
Shelburne Inn	●	50				●				●	●				
Edgewater Inn	●	200				●					●			●	●
Inn At The Market	●	70				●	●							●	●
Alaska Adventurer		15									●	●		●	●
Birchfield Manor	●	10				●	●								
Home by the Sea		14	●	●	●	●				●	●			●	
Inn at Langley	●	30	●	●		●					●			●	
Turtleback Farm Inn												●			

260

SPECIAL INDEXES

	Restaurant open to the public	No. of people for meeting facilities	Kitchens available in some rooms	Fireplaces in some rooms	Facilities for the handicapped	Spas or hot tubs available	Swimming pool on premises	Tennis on premises	Golf available	Horses available	Boating available	Fishing on premises	Children under 12 welcome	Spectacular views	Pets welcome
Western Canada															
Holland House		25		•	•										
Abigails				•		•									
Sooke Harbor House	•	50		•	•	•						•	•	•	•
The Aerie	•	30		•	•	•								•	
Oceanwood Country Inn	•	12	•							•					
Yellow Point Lodge		35		•		•	•	•		•				•	
April Point Lodge	•	120	•	•	•	•			•	•	•	•	•	•	•
Durlacher Hof		20				•			•						
The Park Royal	•	50											•		
Hatheume Lake Lodge		20		•							•	•	•		
Emerald Lake Lodge	•	100		•	•	•				•	•	•		•	
Buffalo Mt Lodge	•	100	•	•	•	•				•			•	•	
Northern Rockies															
River Street Inn						•									•
Idaho Rocky Mt Lodge		150	•	•		•				•		•		•	
Kandahar Lodge		50	•			•						•	•	•	
Flathead Lodge		150					•	•		•	•	•	•	•	
Lone Mountain Lodge	•	60		•		•				•		•	•	•	
Mountain Sky		75		•		•	•	•		•		•	•	•	
Brooks Lake Lodge		50		•	•	•				•	•	•	•	•	
Rusty Parrot		30		•	•	•			•	•	•		•		

261

TRAVELING TO EUROPE?

If your travel plans include a visit to Europe and you would enjoy experiencing the same type of hospitality, service and amenities found in the special Places, we have a recommendation for you.

The International Leading Association

This Belgium based association has over 250 privately owned, high quality lodgings and restaurants in the United Kingdom and throughout the continent. The International Leading Association President is Mr. Richard Cabouret. Richard, an experienced professional in the hotel industry, selects the members, after a through personal inspection.

The Association publishes a beautiful four color guide book listing all the current members. The guide will show you places as diverse as the small "restaurant housed in a 17th Century building well hidden down a tiny street on the left bank" to a secluded all suites hotel in the heart of Knightsbridge. We have picked out one of the colorful boat trips through the French wine country, to be immediately followed by a stay in a villa on the coast of Greece.

If you have enjoyed the Special Places, we are certain you will enjoy discovering these special places of Europe.

For a copy of the guide, contact

Mr. Richard Cabouret

International Leading Association

Rue du Serpentin 33

1050-Bruxelles (Belgium)

Tel: (32) (02) 647 29 23

Fax: (32) (02) 647 43 51

NOTES

TO REORDER

If you would like to order additional copies of Special Places, please use the attached mailing card. If the card has already been used, send your name, address and a personal check for $15.95 plus $1.70 for postage to:

Special Places

P.O. Box 378

Issaquah, WA 98027

(206) 392-0451

FAX (206) 392-7597

PLEASE HELP!

Your reactions to the Special Places are very important to us. Please complete one of the attached post cards after you have experienced one of the places in this edition. Give us your impression of their overall quality, service and attention to your needs. We will then use your information to help us in the on-going process of monitoring each place.

Something Special For You

Each time you send in a postcard (or a letter if your choose) we will enter your name in a quarterly drawing. One prize will be awarded in each of four drawings in January, April, July and October. The prize will be two nights lodging in the Special Place of your choice. To be eligible, entrants must be 21 years of age.

Your Discoveries

Try as we might, we just can not keep up with all the new places. If during your travels you discover a place you feel is quite special, we would appreciate you letting us know. Any suggestions in the 13 western states and two western Canadian provinces will be personally inspected.

Thanks,

Fred and Mardi Nystrom

Special Places

for the discerning traveler

Please send me_____ copies of SPECIAL PLACES® at $15.95 each, plus $1.70 for shipping and handling. Send to:

_____
NAME

_____
ADDRESS

_____
CITY

_____
STATE   ZIP

In

CALIFORNIA, THE PACIFIC NORTHWEST

WESTERN CANADA AND

THE NORTHERN ROCKIES

Special Places

Dear Fred and Mardi,

We experienced the following Special Place:_____
on _____ (Reservation date) and have these comments:

_____

_____

_____

Free Drawing

Enter me in the free quarterly drawing.

_____
Name

_____
Address   City   State/Zip

New Discoveries

We discovered a place we feel is Special and think you should see:

_____

_____

Special Places
P.O. Box 378
Issaquah, WA 98027

Special Places
P.O. Box 378
Issaquah, WA 98027

Special Places

for the discerning traveler

Please send me_____ copies of SPECIAL PLACES® at $15.95 each, plus $1.70 for shipping and handling. Send to:

_____
NAME

_____
ADDRESS

_____
CITY

_____
STATE   ZIP

In

CALIFORNIA, THE PACIFIC NORTHWEST

WESTERN CANADA AND

THE NORTHERN ROCKIES

Special Places

Dear Fred and Mardi,

We experienced the following Special Place:_____
on _____ (Reservation date) and have these comments:

_____

_____

_____

Free Drawing

Enter me in the free quarterly drawing.

_____
Name

_____
Address   City   State/Zip

New Discoveries

We discovered a place we feel is Special and think you should see:

_____

_____

Special Places

P.O. Box 378
Issaquah, WA 98027

Special Places

P.O. Box 378
Issaquah, WA 98027